WARNER BROS. ANIMATION ART

75 YEARS

WARNER BROS.

ENTERTAINING THE WORLD

WARNER BROS.
ANIMATION ART

THE CHARACTERS · THE CREATORS · THE LIMITED EDITIONS

JERRY BECK
and
WILL FRIEDWALD

WORLDWIDE PUBLISHING

Acknowledgments

Jerry Beck and Will Friedwald would like to thank
Andrew J. Lederer, Daniel Goldmark, Keith Scott,
Ruth Clampett, Charles Carney, Greg Ford, Gina Misiroglu,
Hugh Lauter Levin, Jim Muschett, Ken Scaglia, Rebecca
Pranger, Deborah T. Zindell, Victoria Selover, Paul Dini, and
especially our gals, Rose Bevans and Babey.

The publishers wish to thank Linda Jones Clough and her
staff at Linda Jones Enterprises, Steve Felton and Nathan
Gates at Warner Bros. Animation Art, Hope Freleng-Shaw,
The Virgil Ross Trust, Sody Clampett, Robert McKimson, Jr.,
Denise Mayer, Dale Nelson, and Leith Adams.

JACKET ILLUSTRATION: Model Sheets from Bob Clampett Animation Art,
Model Sheet Series, 1991.
(*Page 5*) THAT'S ALL FOLKS! Signed Limited Edition. Friz Freleng, 1989.
(*Page 6*) WHAT'S UP, DOC? Signed Limited Edition. Friz Freleng, 1989.

First published in Great Britain by Virgin Publishing Ltd.
332 Ladbroke Grove
London W10 5AH

© 1997 Warner Bros.
DESIGN: Ken Scaglia
ISBN 1-85227-772-6
PRINTED IN CHINA

A
WARNER BROS. CARTOON

LOONEYTUNES™

™ "WHAT'S UP DOC?"

Contents

CURTAIN CALL. Signed Limited Edition. Chuck Jones, 1994. They know every part by heart: Bugs and Daffy stand ready for their network television debut.

opportunity to carry Warner Bros. art and started ordering signed limited editions as well.

Warner Bros. Classic Animation chief Kathleen Helppie recognized the value and importance of preserving and archiving original production art in the 1980s; meanwhile, collectors had already begun to appreciate the value of original, signed limited-edition cels.

As the sole Warner Bros. licensee, Linda Jones Enterprises (LJE, incorporated in 1981) was the publisher of the first twenty-five limited editions featuring the Warner Bros. characters, each of which was based on an original image drawn by Chuck Jones and each hand-signed by him.

Linda Jones Enterprises approached the great Friz Freleng in 1982 with an offer to publish and distribute his art under LJE's Warner Bros. license. The first eleven Freleng editions were published by LJE. Subsequent editions were published by Freleng's company, by then under license from Warner Bros.

A year later, LJE approached a leading fine art distributor and retailer, Circle Fine Art, with the proposition that Warner Bros. animation art should join the already popular Disney cel art in the company's thirty-four fine art galleries nationwide. The time was propitious and a deal was struck: the beginning of a long and mutually satisfying relationship between an enthusiastic and prominent fine art organization and the limited-edition cel artists.

In 1985, Bob Clampett's widow, Sody, and her family were in the process of starting a scholarship foundation in honor of Clampett's life

DIRECTOR BUGS. Signed Limited Edition. Chuck Jones, 1989. Bugs gives as good as he gets when he's on the other end of the pencil.

work. The Clampetts found it logical to finance the foundation with money raised from the sale of high quality limited-edition cels created from Bob Clampett's films. Although the cels were, of course, unsigned, each carried the family's official endorsement. The publishing business was run by Clampett's daughter, Ruth.

The late director Robert McKimson's family approached LJE with the proposal that limited editions based on McKimson's art be added to the company's publishing schedule. In 1989, the first five McKimson images were published by LJE under its Warner Bros. license. Subsequent editions were produced by the McKimson publishing group under its own Warner Bros. license.

By 1990, Warner Bros. Consumer Products had become interested in the limited-edition phenomenon. LJE published five unsigned limited editions of cels based on Warner Bros.-selected scenes from films by each of the top directors: Tex Avery, Bob Clampett, Friz Freleng, Chuck Jones, and Robert McKimson. The scenes were developed, created, and mastered by Warner Bros. Classic Animation in honor of Bugs Bunny's 50th Anniversary.

The sole Warner Bros. animator (other than animation directors) licensed to enter the limited-edition market was the gentle and talented Virgil Ross. To differentiate animator Ross from the directors' limited editions, Kathleen Helppie developed with Ross the concept of the "sequential series" highlighting the animator's moving images. Backgrounds were realized in colored pencil to help create this distinctive limited-edition style. Warner Bros. granted a license to Ross in 1992. He continued to create images and sign cels until his death in 1996 at the age of 88.

In 1989, Kathleen Helppie and Lorri Bond of Warner Bros. Classic Animation established the Warner Bros. Fine Art Program in support of

WE ARE THE TOONS. Limited Edition. Warner Bros., 1995.

the burgeoning Warner Bros. Studio Store and Gallery business. This program established the Masters Collection, provided seals and certificates of authenticity for classic directors' limited-edition work, framed and distributed the pieces, and created a new standard for consumer security in the purchase of limited editions. This set the policy and procedures which would be instrumental to the establishment of the WB Animation Art Program. Consolidating the (formerly family-run) wholesale distribution process, establishing a vigorous in-house publishing arm of unsigned limited edition cels, and closely monitoring the retail release of animation art, Warner Bros. has continued to support a lively and growing market.

The focus of this book is on limited-edition cel art: art that is carefully and specifically produced for the purpose of supplying the art market. Limited editions created and signed by the artists (Jones, Freleng, and Ross); those editions recreated by family members (Clampett and McKimson), and those produced by staff artists in the tradition and style of the Warner Bros. studio, are all created with the hope that the collector will be touched by a recollection, a moment, a memory inspired by a love of the cartoon characters and the men who created them.

You will find the chapter by Ruth Clampett to be informative and helpful in understanding the process and production of this unique medium. The *catalogue raisonné* at the back of this book brings together, for the first time, a complete visual compendium of the retail limited editions published under the Warner Bros. copyright.

Enjoy!

A Brief History of the Warner Bros. Studios

Warner Bros. Pictures became famous for its gritty depictions of the American experience, wildly entertaining musicals, and the funniest cartoons ever made. Perhaps this should come as no surprise since the Warner brothers themselves—Harry, Albert, Sam, and Jack—led early lives that were as gritty and diverse as their pictures.

The four brothers were born in three different countries: Harry in Poland, Albert and Sam in America, and Jack in Canada. Their parents were often on the move in search of a better life, variously engaged in shoe repair, the grocery business, and the selling of kitchenware to fur trappers. By the turn of the century, this diversity ultimately paid off in the development of the brothers' skills.

Harry, working in the family grocery store, became an astute businessman. Albert, naturally persuasive and assertive, embarked upon a career in sales. Jack, perhaps inspired by the traveling life into which he was born, became a singer. And Sam, who understood the value of ballyhoo, became a carnival barker. When a friend showed Sam a "Kinetoscope," Thomas Edison's pioneering invention for the viewing of motion picture filmstrips, he immediately embraced the possibilities of the mechanism and took a job as a projectionist in Chicago. Enthralled by the wonders of film, he convinced his family to enter the business.

The brothers opened up a storefront "nickelodeon" and exhibited a wide range of moving pictures: slapstick comedies, domestic melodramas, and action-packed Westerns. They divided the responsibilities according to their particular talents—Harry and Albert ran the box office, Sam operated the projector, and Jack sang, the songs illustrated onscreen. Eventually realizing that greater rewards could be gleaned from distributing films than from exhibiting them, the Warners by 1908 were supplying movies to theaters throughout western Pennsylvania.

Movie distribution was becoming big business in the early years of the century, the population obviously delighted to have moving pictures so accessible. The Warners were happy to answer the public's demand and soon were distributing in Virginia and Georgia. Thomas Edison and a handful of other companies possessing early movie patents clearly did not welcome the Warners' entrepreneurship, however, and tried to stop the brothers in their tracks. Determined not to be permanently roadblocked, the Warners turned to production, making a picture called *Peril of the Plains* in a rented studio in St. Louis before joining forces with Universal founder Carl Laemmle in a successful attempt to battle Edison. In 1912 they moved to California and reentered the distribution business.

Warner Bros.' first permanent studio facility was on Sunset Boulevard in Hollywood. This photo, c. 1920, shows the entrance to the Warners' fledgling empire. Jack Warner called this period "the good old days. Positively." Photograph property of Warner Bros.

The Warner Bros. Studios today. Photograph property of Warner Bros.

The Warner brothers: Harry, Jack, Sam, and Albert, 1926. Photograph property of Warner Bros.

Rather than simply exhibit films, the Warner brothers bought the rights to movies and distributed them—a wise financial decision. This newsletter trumpeted the Warners' business acumen to movie house owners. Their next move after exhibition and distribution was a natural: production. Photograph property of Warner Bros.

Once in California, the Warners stepped up their production efforts. They first rented studio space in downtown Los Angeles and Culver City, but it was not long before they built their own lot in Hollywood—the very lot that would ultimately become home to Leon Schlesinger Productions and Warner Bros. Cartoons.

When the studio finally took the name Warner Bros. in 1923, a new era in entertainment history began. In 1925, the Warner brothers, driven by that rare combination of determination and insight that often signals success, managed to acquire the Vitagraph company (which had been a member of the Edison patents trust that had so doggedly opposed their entry into the distribution business), and then purchased the vast Stanley Theaters chain as well as First National Pictures, who were owners of a large Burbank studio which Warner Bros. quickly occupied. The fledgling studio had joined the movie world's major leagues, their new status in no small measure the result of a decision to take a gamble on a new bit of technology—the introduction of sound.

Sam Warner was as intrigued by experiments in movie sound as he had been by movie projection itself. He convinced Harry, who was running the business end of the company, to engage the studio in a partnership with Western Electric to be called The Vitaphone Corporation. Synchronizing sound to picture—keeping the suspense in every cliffhanger and the romance in every tear-jerker—was no small task, but Vitaphone was determined to solve these problems, and was ultimately able to link disk and projection systems successfully. At first, Vitaphone technology was used mainly for music and effects, but synchronization also allowed motion pictures to talk. When Al Jolson spoke and sang during the sound sequences of Warners' 1927 *The Jazz*

Sam (second from right) and Jack (far right) took their films on "Road Shows" from city to city, exhibiting them and promoting their business along the way. This photo and its notation are from Jack Warner's personal scrapbook. Photograph property of Warner Bros.

Singer, silent movies were silenced forever, and Warner Bros. vaulted to the front of a new technological field.

Tragically, Sam Warner died on the eve of *The Jazz Singer*'s release. From this point on, Warner Bros. was essentially run by Jack and Harry, with Harry supervising financial matters in New York while Jack supervised studio production in Los Angeles. (Jack was not too busy, however, with the demands of the rapidly expanding studio to give up his gig at the studio's radio station, KFWB, where he still sang under his old stage name, Leon Zuardo.) By 1930, Warner Bros.' popular "Vitaphone Shorts" included a new animated series called Looney Tunes, which featured a fully sound-synchronized character named Bosko, the first of many animation luminaries to come. Warner, thanks to its newest brainchild of sound-synchronization, was in a full production schedule and has remained at the forefront of the motion picture industry ever since.

It was a golden era for Warner Bros. With America (and the rest of the world) on the verge of a major economic depression, the movies provided an inexpensive diversion—if only for a couple of hours. Warner Bros. battled the effects of the Depression with two trademark genres— extravagant musicals that made the public forget their problems and realistic social dramas that helped them confront them. Seemingly "ripped from the headlines," dramas like *I Am A Fugitive From A Chain Gang, The Public Enemy*, and *Little Caesar* uncompromisingly reflected the injustice and deprivation of the day. On the other hand, choreographer Busby Berkeley's elaborate production numbers in musicals like *42nd Street*, the *"Gold Diggers"* series, and *Dames* could lighten even the heaviest load in the whirl of kaleidoscopic imagery and arresting camera angles unprecedented in the genre. In 1931 Looney Tunes spawned a second series of animated cartoons, Merrie Melodies, which was designed to popularize Warner's burgeoning music catalogue.

Warner's animated stars were by no means the only ones in the studio's constellation. Bette Davis, Edward G. Robinson, and James Cagney brought grit and "attitude" to the screen and became stars whose names and faces have become inextricably linked with the Warner Bros. shield. Dick Powell and Ruby Keeler charmed an entire nation with their youthful idealism and playful romantic escapades. And Errol Flynn swashbuckled across landscapes both black-and-white and Technicolor in the service of his fair maiden, Olivia de Havilland. The Warners' roster even included a future American president by the name of Ronald Reagan, who convincingly played both Everyman and Everyhero. And

Warner Bros. presented "Classics of the Screen" to theater owners across the country. Since they couldn't afford movie stars early on, the brothers bought the rights to books, which they made into films. Jack (far left) and Sam (far right) promoted the films on their Road Shows, with exhibits such as this on a flatbed truck. Photograph property of Warner Bros.

(*Left*) Warner contract player Edward G. Robinson became a huge star through his roles as a movie tough guy. Photograph property of Warner Bros.

(*Above*) Cagney's menacing charm electrified audiences in *The Public Enemy* (1931). Photograph property of Warner Bros.

Warner's leading men and ladies were supported by a stock company of actors including idiosyncratic characters like Ned Sparks and Zasu Pitts, and perennial sidekicks Allen Jenkins and Frank McHugh whose abilities to be foil or friend helped make the studio a box-office leader.

The 1940s ushered in the end of worldwide depression and the beginning of worldwide war. Warner answered the bugle call with patriotic films like *Across the Pacific*, *Destination Tokyo*, and *Mission to Moscow*. Stalwart Humphrey Bogart finally became a full-fledged star with movies like *High Sierra*, *The Maltese Falcon*, and *Casablanca*, all films that pitted a hero in a battle of conscience. Warner's most notable, and perhaps most memorable, continuing character, though, was cartoon star Bugs Bunny, born in 1940, whose defiant defense of his own turf became synonymous with the American war effort. Bugs was so popular in the 1940s that he became one of the first "multi-media" stars, cavorting across cartoons and feature films alike, appearing with comic actor Jack Carson in *Two Guys from Texas* and *My Dream is Yours*.

The late 1940s brought about the end of the studio era that Warner Bros. had helped to create. The government, as part of its post-war efforts

to decentralize, felt that studios like Warner Bros. that not only produced and distributed, but also exhibited films in their theaters, had an unfair marketplace advantage. So after years of prodding, the major studios finally agreed, in 1948, to divest themselves of their theater chains, which were then broken up into separate companies.

Warner Bros. was no longer involved with the exhibition end of the movie business, but the studio was quick to pick up the slack elsewhere. In the 1950s, bigger-budget and wider-screen feature films (even a brief detour into 3-D) drew in the crowds. James Dean and Doris Day emerged as big-screen stars and icons of the era. Warner Bros., by 1955 a powerful presence in the entertainment industry, typically inaugurated the studio's entry into what would become another spectacularly successful enterprise—television production—becoming the first major movie studio to cast its lot with the networks. Television production shifted from the east coast to the west, and shows like "Cheyenne," "Maverick," "77 Sunset Strip," and "Sugarfoot"—not to mention "The Bugs Bunny Show" (in 1960)—gave the small ABC network a prominence it had never before enjoyed.

One classic Warner Bros. film followed another in the 1960s—films like *The Music Man*, *My Fair Lady*, and *Who's Afraid of Virginia Woolf?* In 1967, the year of *Camelot*, *Bonnie and Clyde*, and *Cool Hand Luke*, Warner Bros. was sold to a Canadian company called Seven Arts, and was renamed Warner Bros.-Seven Arts for the remainder of the decade. Two years later, Warners was acquired by Steven Ross's Kinney National Service (renamed Warner Communications), under whose logo the venerable giant was brought into the modern era. That same year also marked the end of the classic short subject era of Warner Bros. theatrical cartoons, at least for a time.

(*Above, left*) A gathering of legends: (standing, left to right) Jack Warner, actor Paul Muni, director William Dieterle, and producer Hal Wallis; (seated, left to right) director Cecil B. DeMille, Charles Chaplin, author H.G. Wells. Photograph property of Warner Bros.

(*Above, right*) Jack Warner in a studio shot reminiscent of those taken of his stars, c. 1930. Photograph property of Warner Bros.

Under Ross, Warner Communications enjoyed a new period of stability and growth: its dominance of the music business was secured, and its entry into cable TV offered seemingly limitless opportunities for the future as new developments in communications literally brought the world to everyone's doorstep. Warner Communications engineered a 1989 merger with publishing giant Time Inc., and the new offspring, Time Warner Inc., became an industry leader in every aspect of media. From 1989 to1995, Warner Bros. Television Animation created two powerful new series—"Tiny Toon Adventures" and "Animaniacs"—whose huge success on the Fox Network further defined the animation studio as an industry powerhouse. In 1995, Warner Bros. finally got its own television network with the launch of The WB and its Kids' WB! animated cartoon component, and immediately became a powerful force in children's television as well. The company's acquisition of Turner Broadcasting System, Inc., in 1996 brought a huge list of Warner Bros. films and cartoons, which had been sold by Jack Warner to television distributor Associated Artists Productions (A.A.P.) in the 1950s, back to their original home, giving Warners the largest catalog of film history ever.

Today Time Warner encompasses feature films, television, book and magazine publishing, animated cartoons, cable networks, theme parks, music, consumer products, home video, retail stores, and much, much more—a portfolio of activities no less diverse than those in which Warner Bros. founders Harry, Albert, Sam, and Jack Warner engaged so many decades ago. The legacy of the Warner brothers themselves will no doubt continue well into the next century via the activities of the company that was created in their image and still carries their name.

The Warners also owned radio station KFWB, which was broadcast live across the country. In this 1931 photo, Jack Warner (left of the microphone) poses with some of his famous colleagues, including Joe E. Brown (in double-breasted suit), Edward G. Robinson (in costume for *Silver Dollar*), Mervyn LeRoy (behind Robinson), Ruby Keeler (in stole), and Paul Muni (in prison garb, directly from the day's filming of *I Am A Fugitive From A Chain Gang*). Photograph property of Warner Bros.

The Dawn of Hollywood Animation

Watch me move!" shouts a character in Winsor McCay's 1911 *Little Nemo*, one of the first animated films. That single declaration distills the astonishing novelty of early animation into one bold statement: through the magic of cinema, not only could photographs move, but now, even drawings could come to life. Animation—which is to say, drawings in motion—actually predates the existence of both photography and cinema by several centuries. All manner of precinematic devices, from flip books to magic lanterns to praxinoscopes, were used to breathe life into the artist's creation long before even the first photographic daguerreotype. But there was no magic as powerful as the magic that happened when animation met film in the early 1900s.

Movement itself was the major attraction of early cinema, whether live or animated. However, the single most important element of animation in its first three decades was its proximity to a medium far more popular than film itself at the turn of the century—the comic strip. Throughout its history, the animated cartoon has always maintained a close connection with its newspaper cousin, and that relationship was never closer than during the silent era. Both comic and cartoon used funny drawings to convey humor, both tickled audiences of all ages, and, most importantly, both mediums sprung from the remarkably creative—and necessarily slightly wacky—mind of a singular artist/creator. Animated film was clearly born of the world of comics.

Early in the century, it was not unusual for newspaper cartoonists to pack their bags and head out on the vaudeville circuit. Paper, an easel, and a piece of chalk were all they needed to amuse an audience with "chalk-talk" drawings and "lightning sketches" of their famous comic characters. Enter cartoonist J. Stuart Blackton, the first to try combining drawings and film. In 1900, his live-action "trick film" *The Enchanted Drawing* has Blackton interacting with his still drawings by pulling objects out of his sketches, which become the "real" article. Obviously intrigued by these new "tricks," Blackton continued to experiment with film during the next few years, culminating in his landmark film *Humorous Phases Of Funny Faces* in 1906, a chalk-talk come to life, with chalk-drawn characters moving, albeit crudely, to illustrate a few (even cruder) jokes.

Frenchman Emile Cohl took animated cartoons further with his *Fantoches* (1908), which had stick figures, drawn on paper, metamorphose and move. But it was famed cartoonist Winsor McCay who in 1911 caught the attention of pioneering cartoonists in New York when he

Some of the founders of Hollywood animation, from a 1927 photo. From left to right: Friz Freleng, Walker Harman, Walt Disney, Margie Gay, Rudolf Ising, Ub Iwerks, Hugh Harman, and Roy Disney.

brought his comic strip characters to life in the short animated film *Little Nemo*. Like its predecessors, *Little Nemo* was created to delight vaudeville audiences, but its exquisite artwork and "full" animation was seminal and offered a glimpse at the possibilities inherent in this new medium.

McCay followed *Nemo* with two other films, *The Story Of A Mosquito* (1912) and *Gertie The Dinosaur* (1914), each one taking over a year of painstaking work by McCay and his assistant. Gertie was a truly remarkable reptile—an original character with a real personality—and the film proved to be McCay's most influential early effort.

Cartoonists were not the only ones to move animation along. An astute businessman takes notice of what makes people happy, and it wasn't long before publisher William Randolph Hearst began putting his popular comics stars in animated films. In 1914, his was the first animation studio created to take popular comic strip characters off of the newspaper page and put them on the screen as part of motion picture newsreels. Comic strips had become so popular by the turn of the century that characters like Krazy Kat, Mutt & Jeff, and Buster Brown were as important to circulation as anyone on the payroll. Little wonder they were among the first animated for the screen.

J. R. Bray, Earl Hurd, Max Fleischer, and Paul Terry were among the growing ranks of New York newspaper cartoonists who were anxious to take this emerging art form even further. Bray and Hurd used sheets of celluloid to speed production of animated cartoons, Bray devising a method of drawing the background on a stationary cel that could be used over and over, and Hurd reversing this process by drawing the characters

on cels, which were then laid over a painted background. This method of production, patented by Bray & Hurd, remains the industry standard today for cel animation.

Before 1920, Fleischer and Terry had taken the established factory-system techniques and combined them with new characters and clever invention to create two of the brightest cartoon series of the silent era: Fleischer's *Out of the Inkwell* and Terry's *Aesop's Fables*. Max Fleischer's invention, the rotoscope (a means of tracing live action for animation), introduced Ko-Ko The Klown in the *Inkwell* series and pioneered the novel combination of rotoscope and squash-and-stretch animation (a fine example of which is the rotoscoped rendering of Uncle Sam paired with the conventionally animated Porky Pig in the 1939 Warner Bros. cartoon *Old Glory*, directed by Chuck Jones). Fleischer's studio went on to create the instantly popular "bouncing ball" sing-along cartoons, and in the sound era brought the likes of Popeye, Betty Boop, and Superman to the screen.

Paul Terry gave Aesop's Fables a whole new look. Zany animal antics told the tale, and each film ended with a written punchline telling the moral of the story that usually drew more laughter than the cartoon itself. Quality of drawings didn't matter then; quantity of action and quality of humor did. Silent cartoons caught on with moviegoers, and the animated subjects were soon lifted out of the newsreel and became their own seven-minute subjects.

Animated shorts, now a bona fide genre, produced their own group of stars—Pat Sullivan's Felix the Cat (created by Otto Messmer and certainly the most popular animated star of the 1920s), Walter Lantz's Dinky Doodle, and Walt Disney's Oswald The Lucky Rabbit, to name but a few.

Once the techniques and methods of production were established, little progress was made in the field of animated cartoons between 1918 and 1928. But in 1926, the Warner brothers introduced a device that would soon revolutionize cartoons and all motion pictures—the Vitaphone—which successfully synchronized prerecorded sound. The following year, Warner Bros.' *The Jazz Singer* debuted talking movies, heralding a new era for motion pictures.

By 1928, all-talkie movie programs were filling theaters, and a young Walt Disney decided to take a gamble on a sound cartoon. Mickey Mouse, the star of Disney's *Steamboat Willie*, became an overnight sensation;

within a year every major movie studio added sound cartoons to their release schedules. Warner Bros.' short-subject producer Leon Schlesinger followed suit and contracted with former Disney animators, Hugh Harman, Rudolf Ising, and Friz Freleng to create a new series of musical cartoons, Looney Tunes.

LAST OF THE DO-DOS. Limited Edition. Bob Clampett, 1991. Porky catches what he thinks is the "last of the Do-Dos," the last scene before the iris in Clampett's *Porky in Wackyland* (1938).

The Creation of Looney Tunes and Merrie Melodies

Veteran animator Shamus Culhane, talking to animation historian Leonard Maltin in a 1967 interview about his stint as head of Paramount's failing animation department, lamented that "the sales department was a bunch of fat, cigar-chewing gentlemen who frequently asked, 'Why can't you give us something like Bugs Bunny?' I tried to explain that Bugs Bunny didn't come about because somebody said, 'Let's make Bugs Bunny.' It happened almost by accident, to find a character who was a good actor. It just happened—you couldn't order one."

Great characters do not start out fully formed, nor does a great series of cartoons. Artists and writers try their best and, if given time to develop their art, may bring about something which transcends the sum of all the creative energy that has gone into the work. This was true not only for the remarkable Warner Bros. cartoon characters, but for their creators and the entire string of Looney Tunes and Merrie Melodies. Ideas flourished in the hands of their creators and became legend.

Animated cartoons were an expected part of standard movie fare in 1930. Depression-era audiences felt cheated if, in addition to a feature film, they didn't see a cartoon, a newsreel, a short comedy, "preview flashes," and perhaps a travelogue, serial chapter, or musical short subject. Instantly popular, the theatrical cartoon continued as a staple of the movie-going experience into the mid-1960s, surviving sky-rocketing production costs and expanding technology (mainly television) that did away with all the other "selected" short subjects of Hollywood's golden age.

By 1930, every major studio (in response to a public that clearly delighted in animated antics) had aligned itself with a cartoon producer or created its own in-house animation studio. Warner Bros. commenced Looney Tunes in 1930 and, quick on the heels of its success, debuted a second series, Merrie Melodies, in 1931. Leon Schlesinger Productions contracted with directors Hugh Harman and Rudolf Ising, and a young animator named Isadore "Friz" Freleng, to bring them to life.

Harman and Ising began their careers around 1922 at Kansas City Film Ad, a Missouri advertising house that also employed an ambitious and visionary young cartoonist named Walt Disney. When Disney began producing rudimentary animated films for local theaters, his colleagues joined him. The two stuck with the young entrepreneur throughout the earliest stages of his career: Disney's live-action/animation *Alice* comedies, his move to California in the mid-1920s, and his all-animated *Oswald The Lucky Rabbit* series. By now, Freleng (another refugee from Kansas City Film Ad) had been persuaded to join the group.

While never the subject of a limited edition cel, Bosko and his many moods (mainly happy-go-lucky) are reflected in this studio model sheet from 1930.

When, at the very end of the silent era, Disney entered into a dispute with his distributor, Charles Mintz, the studio split into two factions. Some members went with Disney and Ub Iwerks to work on what would become the first Mickey Mouse cartoons. Others, most notably animator and future directing giant Freleng, remained with Harman, Ising, and Mintz to continue production on the *Oswald* series. However, Harman and Ising soon found themselves out in the cold when Mintz lost the rights to the Oswald character, which went to Universal and Walter Lantz.

Fortunately, 1929 was a good year to be in the cartoon business; virtually every major studio in Hollywood wanted a piece of the action that Disney was creating with the first sound cartoons. Harman and Ising, determined to make it on their own, produced a test film called *Bosko The TalkINK Kid*. While Disney's early animated action had been merely synchronized to music, Harman and Ising took sound animation a step further; Bosko actually spoke *and* sang, thanks to Freleng's pioneering dialogue animation. The Warner brothers, who had originally sponsored the invention of the talking film, took notice and contracted two separate series of one-reel cartoons from Harman, Ising, and Freleng via Schlesinger, both following patterns established by Disney in 1928 and 1929. The first Looney Tunes cartoon, *Sinkin' In The Bathtub*, animated by Friz Freleng, was a popular success. The Looney Tunes series would star Bosko and a regular cast, while the Merrie Melodies, a series begun a year later, featured no recurring character and would serve primarily to promote songs owned by the Warner's various publishing wings.

Harman and Ising have often been thought of as mere Disney imitators. But, in fact, any similarities that might be noted between Disney and his fellow Missourians are largely because they all shared a Midwest background and silent-era training.

Blessed with a serendipitously harmonious company name, the Harman-Ising partnership did their best work with music. The Bosko cartoons, featuring the diminutive hero confronted with slightly different situations in each new episode, and the Merrie Melodies, which used different characters and settings but virtually the same plot (involving a boy, a girl, and a villain) in each reel, were spirited along by music that kept audiences glued to the action. Even in their best films, Harman and Ising traditionally ignored plot and character development in order to concentrate on musical movement, resulting in such exuberant efforts as *A Great Big Bunch of You* and the surreal Freleng-Norm Blackburn-animated *You Don't Know What You're Doin'*, both of which pivot around some of the brightest, most irresistible song-and-dance sequences ever animated.

Indeed, when Harman, Ising, and Freleng left Schlesinger and Warner Bros. in 1993 to start their own company, the studio found it hard to maintain the same "standards" that H & I had established. At first, the best Schlesinger could manage (in 1933) was a character called Buddy, who has been charitably referred to as "Bosko in whiteface." While Schlesinger's early color efforts resulted in some snappy musicals, like Earl Duvall's *Honeymoon Hotel*, the studio seemed intent upon working within the creative confines of past successes. But in 1934, Freleng was called back by Schlesinger to direct. Warner cartoons were now back on track.

Between 1936 and 1938, two talented young animators began working their way up the production ladders, from assistants to animators to directors. Friz Freleng, Tex Avery, and Frank Tashlin, who were already directing by 1936, were joined by Bob Clampett and Chuck Jones, who emerged as directors (or "supervisors") during this three-year interval. Through uninterrupted production—an average of three dozen films a year in the late 1930s—and constant experimentation, the familiar Warner Bros. trademarks began to take shape. The "screwball" comedy was the hallmark film of the late Depression era, and Warner Bros. kept up the pace, with one cartoon faster than the last.

Then too, the Warner cartoonists were much more concerned with topicality than their Disney counterparts, and their writers were considerably quicker to pick up on running gags and trends from popular feature films and radio programs. While Disney strived for timelessness, the Looney Tunesmiths revelled in timeliness, incorporating appearances by everyone from Jimmy Durante to Adolf Hitler. Thanks to musical genius Carl W. Stalling, sound effects wizard

Assistant animators Madilyn and Marilyn Wood were identical twins. 1952. Photograph property of Warner Bros.

The painting process. Photograph property of Warner Bros.

The cels are polished before being photographed to remove fingerprints, dust, and other smudges that will show up on camera. Photograph property of Warner Bros.

Friz Freleng's animation unit, 1940, at Leon Schlesinger
Studio: (front row, left to right) Les Larson, Dave Brown,
Constantin Lebedef, Manuel Perez, Herman Cohen, Bob
Matz; (back row, left to right) Dick Thompson (leaning over
John Kennedy), Cal Dalton, Sam Nicholson, Ken Champin,
Leonard Kester, Gerry Chiniquy, Dick Bickenbach, Al Tarter,
Gil Turner, and Friz Freleng in his fedora. Photograph
property of Warner Bros.

Treg Brown, and voice artist *par excellence* Mel Blanc, the Warner
cartoons even had their own distinctive audio identity.

But the main reason that the Warner cartoons became the funniest
in Hollywood history was the unprecedented (and, some say,
unintentional) freedom afforded their creators by executive producer
Leon Schlesinger. Schlesinger owned and allegedly operated the studio,
but felt no need to have a hand in its every aspect. As long as the output
was funny and profitable, Schlesinger was happy. Free to develop their
own distinctive styles, Freleng, Avery, Clampett, Jones, Robert
McKimson, and Tashlin eventually came to be regarded as the greatest
talents in the history of cartoon comedy (with Norm McCabe and Art
Davis not far behind). And there's no environment that could have
nurtured these talents so keenly as the beaten-down building that they
lovingly referred to as "Termite Terrace."

Freleng, who had been with the studio from the start, was the
creative "pointman," and his lively hand, which guided an astonishing
group of artistic talents, allowed comic wild cards like Tex Avery to come
aboard as director and develop many of the signature components of both
his (and what was becoming the studio's) style—the breakneck pacing,
the wiseguy attitude, the audacity, and the sheer outrageousness. Avery
was also determined to take the theatrical convention known as
"suspension of disbelief" and turn it on its ear by continually underscoring
the artificiality of his characters as well as the cinematic process (having
characters directly address the audience, for example).

Other directors took Avery's ideas and ran with them while

Freleng responded and sharpened the Warner cartoons' style and added his own touch, beginning with the Merrie Melodies, the studio's ongoing series of song-driven musicals. Picking up on the greater flexibility allowed by Warner's newfound irreverence, Freleng by 1937 had abandoned the fluid, sinuous motion of the earlier melodies and turned to more satirical comic timing (*She Was An Acrobat's Daughter*), evocations of pure speed (the dodge-and-weave car animation of *Streamlined Greta Green*), and gags which more ambitiously encompassed the entire field of the frame (*The Fella With A Fiddle*). Freleng's raucous and determinedly anti-cute *The Lyin' Mouse* confirmed the director's contribution to the growth of Warner's wacky rowdyism. That's by bold, broad strokes as well as by subtler (though no less insidious) means.

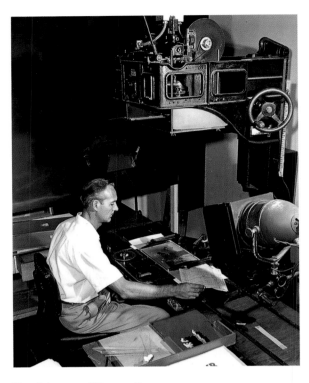

Ken Moore, a Warner Bros. cartoon cameraman, shoots each cel over a painted background, with a specially designed animation camera. 1952. Photograph property of Warner Bros.

The cagey sense of timing on display in his well-known forays into classical music (*Rhapsody In Rivets*, *Pigs In A Polka*, *Holiday For Shoestrings*, *Mouse Mazurka*) finally set the tone for all the studio's like-minded ventures to follow. It's Freleng's outrageous experiments in musical synchronization that cracked the door for such later Jones-directed masterworks as *Long-Haired Hare* and *Rabbit of Seville*. But Freleng's impeccable timing would be equally at play in all of his 266 or so classic cartoons. He invented definitive cartoon antagonists like Sylvester (in 1945's *Life With Feathers*) and Yosemite Sam (in the same year's *Hare Trigger*). But whether it's Sylvester v. Tweety or Yosemite Sam v. Bugs, the timing of each gag was everything, set to the director's internal metronome.

Another talent who came along in the mid-1930s was Frank Tashlin, who launched his future career as a live-action director with a series of stylishly ambitious masterpieces. Tashlin's cinematic aspirations were clear from the beginning. In efforts like *Porky's Romance* (1937), *Porky In The North Woods* (1936), and *The Case Of The Stuttering Pig* (1937), "Tash" (or "Tish-Tash," as he was sometimes billed) used all manner of cross-cutting, wipes, dissolves, montage, and other devices rarely seen in a cartoon context. After working on a brace of some of the finest Porky Pig cartoons and Merrie Melodies, the talented Mr. Tish-Tash left the studio, but thankfully returned during its zenith in the war years. He then supplied Warner with some of its funniest efforts of its greatest period—especially *The Swooner Crooner*—and showed a particular talent for his own incarnation of Daffy Duck in *Plane Daffy*, *Stupid Cupid*, *Porky Pig's Feat*, and *Nasty Quacks*. In 1946, Tashlin said goodbye to the studio for the last time and found fame in live-action film.

Of all post-Avery stylists, Bob Clampett remained truest to Tex's vision, yet he too clearly made his own mark on the industry. While Avery had been one of the "midwives" to the birth of Bugs and Daffy, ultimately character-driven films were not for him as they became for Freleng and, later, Chuck Jones. As Avery further illustrated in the 1940s

and 1950s at MGM, he'd rather revel in the artificiality of an animated entity than have it induce sympathy. Clampett, however, was too much of a ham actor himself to make anything more important than his stars. He developed the duck and the rabbit into screen personalities made endearing despite their ridiculously hyperbolized pugnacity. Clampett also exalted in exposing the latent antisocial tendencies of the ultracute, such as his creation of the baby-like Tweety in his early films and the infantile Bugs in *The Old Grey Hare*. Clampett's explosive, maniacal machinations became, like Freleng's timing and Jones's wit, legend.

Robert McKimson (and Clampett) will forever be credited for literally shaping the look of Bugs Bunny into the character audiences know and love today. After Bugs's introduction in *A Wild Hare*, McKimson, as an animator under Clampett's direction, began the process of revising Bugs's look, from the oval-faced rabbit of the Avery cartoon to the softer-muzzled, longer toothed, and more expressive Bugs of the Clampett cartoons of the early 1940s. Soon, all the directors at Warner Bros. cartoons adapted the McKimson Bugs to their individual style. As a director, McKimson would also expand upon the character's joyous sense of anarchy in some of Bugs's most raucous performances.

Chuck Jones's touch was immediately recognizable; his films presented a particularly handsome drawing style and a distinct sensitivity, from his deliberately precious, Disney-flavored early work to the intensity of his fast and furious chases amid seemingly endless cliffs and explosions in the 1950s Road Runner films. Through it all, Jones was a master of nuance, which allowed him to reconceive Bugs Bunny as cool and Daffy Duck as despicable. Widely read and eminently quotable, Jones has since become animation's resident intellectual—although none of his cartoons are so cerebral that they sacrifice the delicious lunacy that tickles even the most stalwart of viewers.

Any mention of the Looney Tunes/Merrie Melodies cartoonists would be incomplete without recognizing the other essential element of the studio's success—namely the character boom that began in the late 1930s. After struggling with the passive Bosko and Buddy for five years, the studio quickly debuted the big three—Porky Pig, Daffy Duck, and, at last, Bugs Bunny—between 1935 and 1940. Freleng directed Porky's first appearance in *I Haven't Got A Hat* (1935). By the following year, the pantless pig had asserted himself as the studio's first long-lasting star and was already becoming an icon in the evolution of the Hollywood cartoon. Like Mickey before him, Porky was an essentially noncommittal Everypig placed in a variety of situations. Like Bosko and Buddy (whom he replaced as star of the studio's black-and-white Looney Tunes), he had a girlfriend, Petunia Pig, who arrived in 1937, and a succession of dogs. What set Porky and friends apart were their situations, which drew more and more on the increasingly irreverent and eventually wacky sensibilities of the Warner's studio. This was never more so than when Porky stumbled onto the story formula that would soon define the Warner cartoon: the hunting picture.

The recurring-character Looney Tunes were certainly not the studio's only hotbed of activity in the late 1930s. Hollywood was using color, and Warner followed suit in its omnibus cartoon series, the Merrie Melodies, which were largely Freleng's domain. While the black-and-white Porky shorts became more involved with plot, the color Merrie Melodies continued to concentrate on music and the Harman-Ising tradition of building films around songs. It seemed inevitable that the same zany spirit that drove the Looney Tunes would soon penetrate the Merrie Melodies, and it did when Avery graduated to the more prestigious color reels, such as *I Only Have Eyes For You* (1937). Frank Tashlin also left his own stamp on the studio's musicals by perfecting another subgenre pioneered by Harman-Ising, the book-covers-come-to-life format. Tashlin's three variations on the theme—*Speaking of the Weather* (1937), *You're An Education* (1938), and *Have You Got Any Castles* (1938)—feature all manner of topical gags and engaging animated action, each cartoon featuring a medley of well-known songs. Avery enlivened the Melodies further with a subseries of plotless newsreel and travelogue parodies, beginning with *The Isle of Pingo Pongo* (1938) and climaxing with the Oscar-nominated *Detouring America* (1939).

Meanwhile, back in the black-and-whites, Porky Pig's star, which had begun to rise when he left his original *I Haven't Got A Hat* troupe behind, was eventually eclipsed by two new players, Daffy Duck and Bugs Bunny. In *Porky's Duck Hunt* (1937), the Pig goes hunting and encounters a screwy adversary named Daffy Duck. In Tex Avery's 1940 short *A Wild Hare*, Elmer Fudd goes hunting and encounters a rabbit—Bugs Bunny, an equally if not more challenging prey than Daffy.

By the early 1940s, all the elements of the Warner style were in place, and even the departure of Avery in 1942 (followed by Tashlin and then Clampett in 1946) could not stop the relentless juggernaut of cartoon high-comedy that the studio had set into motion, especially when driven by the extraordinary animation talents of Bob McKimson (who was soon to become a director), Ken Harris, and Virgil Ross, among many others. By World War II, Bugs Bunny had become by far the most popular animated icon of the era—possibly of all time. Just as Mickey Mouse's cheerfulness had spoken to America during the Great Depression, Bugs's brashness, bravura, and Brooklyn accent were a welcome tonic for a nation at war. Indeed, it was the "wabbit's" very Americanness that made him a perfect world traveler in the post-war era, visiting locales from Scotland (in *My Bunny Lies Over The Sea*) to the African desert (in *Sahara Hare*). He was the standard-bearer for the Looney Tunes cast, further supporting the studio through licensing, appearing on every

product from comic books to clothing. By the late 1940s, Bugs was so universally loved that his incredible screen presence was enlisted, in special animated-live action sequences directed by Freleng, to perk up interest in Warner's features *My Dream Is Yours* and *Two Guys From Texas*.

Ultimately, it was the overwhelming international success of Bugs Bunny that probably convinced the front office that producing rather than simply owning and distributing this highly profitable rabbit and his films would be a sound economic move. In 1944, Warner Bros. bought out all of Schlesinger's interests. According to director Chuck Jones, Edward Selzer, who was appointed to take Schlesinger's place as studio supervisor, shared several of his predecessor's qualities: like Leon, he knew little about film production, animation, or comedy. But unlike Schlesinger, he was unable to resist the temptation to interfere with his creative staff's work, which, of course, meant *war*. It is oft-repeated studio lore that Jones's classic *Bully for Bugs* originated with Selzer's incongruous pronouncement that bullfights were *not* funny.

In the early "Warner" era, the Bugs and Daffy films launched an arresting array of foils and co-stars, from Elmer Fudd to Yosemite Sam and, later, the Tasmanian Devil. As the decade wore on, other series got

A WILD HARE. Limited Edition. Warner Bros. Classic Animation, 1990. In a mighty hop, Bugs Bunny is born, and the world hasn't been the same since. Neither has Elmer Fudd.

underway which had been similarly inspired by Bugs and Daffy's chase-and-hunt format, including Tweety and Sylvester, Foghorn Leghorn, the Road Runner and Wile E. Coyote, and Pepé Le Pew (the latter being the only animated entity whose chases were motivated by amorous rather than carnivorous intent). As always, these were all born of experimentation—with the development of individual character traits or the play of one character off another. Robert McKimson's creation, Foghorn Leghorn, was conceived as a sparring partner for Henery Hawk but quickly stole the show from the half-pint hen-stealer. Freleng arrived at the masterstroke of pairing up Clampett's Tweety and his own Sylvester and playing up their exquisite dynamic, which carried through dozens of rematches over three decades.

The decision to unite cat with canary was so monumental, in fact, that in 1948 Freleng won an Academy Award for *Tweetie Pie,* Warner Bros. animation studio's first Oscar. The statuette for best short cartoon was first presented in 1932, and for the next decade Disney brought it home so often that it was practically known as "The Uncle Walt Award." While Warner began receiving nominations regularly in 1939, there was a certain randomness regarding the Academy's choices. The first Warner cartoon short of this period to be nominated was Avery's *Detouring America* (1939), a funny but unspectacular travelogue parody; the second was the same director's *A Wild Hare,* the classic that defined Elmer and in which Bugs Bunny debuted. Warner finally bagged the trophy with Freleng's aforementioned 1947 *Tweetie Pie.* As it happened, the award similarly served to signify the Academy's blessing for other new characters, such as Pepé Le Pew, in his fourth appearance (*For Scentimental Reasons,* 1949) and *Speedy Gonzales,* in his second (1955). Freleng's masterwork *Birds Anonymous* (1957) may mark the only time a genuine Warner's classic won the prize (classics like *One Froggy Evening* and *What's Opera, Doc?* were ignored). When Freleng finally took home the trophy for a medieval-era hare-and-Yosemite Sam entry (*Knighty Knight Bugs,* 1958), it was clear that the Academy was not only honoring an outstanding individual performance but also giving the Rabbit a lifetime achievement award (one for which he had campaigned very vocally in Clampett's 1944 short *What's Cookin' Doc?*). The animators themselves knew that their cartoons had become the most popular animated shorts ever made, and they entered the 1950s fertile with lots of new gags.

The 1950s was the decade in which the work of Chuck Jones would flourish. Though an animator since the mid-1930s and a director since 1937, Jones did not accomplish his best work until the beginning of the 1950s. But after almost a decade and a half at the studio, he directed a string of classics that have stood the test of time and which, for many, serve to define the Warner Bros. cartoon.

I Say, I Say, Son... Limited Edition. Robert McKimson, 1993. Foghorn Leghorn stole the show from Henery Hawk in his first cartoon (*Walky Talky Hawky*, directed by McKimson) by not letting the little guy get a word in edgewise. Unfortunately for Foghorn, the Barnyard Dawg knows how to get through to him.

Jones's unique combination of modern graphics and subtle personality animation further broadened and certainly deepened the personalities of Bugs Bunny, Daffy Duck, and Porky Pig. His Bugs-and-Daffy classics established a relationship fraught with psychological nuance that was almost Freudian in its acuity. He made the world of opera more accessible to a mass audience with *What's Opera, Doc?* and *Rabbit of Seville*. Jones, along with layout artist Maurice Noble, created an outer-space milieu in epics like *Duck Dodgers in the 24 1/2th Century* that influenced today's big-budget sci-fi filmmakers. And his *One Froggy Evening* starred a frustrating musical frog who ended up some forty years later as the moving icon for Warner Bros.' entire television network.

Adding to the now-classic adversarial marriage of Bugs and Daffy was Freleng's 1957 *Show Biz Bugs*. The cartoon featured Freleng's familiar vaudevillian themes, but now these gags punctuated the intensely competitive Bugs/Daffy relationship established by Jones, and extended the explosive war of words-and-action that Friz had cleverly devised for Bugs and Yosemite Sam and now applied to Bugs and Daffy. Whether intentionally or not, *Show Biz Bugs*, with its variety show depiction of the cartoon unit's top stars, laid the conceptual groundwork for the wrap-arounds of "The Bugs Bunny Show," the studio's first foray into network television.

(*Above*) June Foray and Mel Blanc take direction from animation director Chuck Jones in a voice session rehearsal, c. 1957. Photograph property of Warner Bros.

(*Left*) A publicity shot, c. 1957, of a gathering of animation legends. Writer Michael Maltese presents a storyboard to (first row, back to front) directors Chuck Jones and Friz Freleng, producer Edward Selzer, Selzer's secretary; (second row, back to front) writer Tedd Pierce, director Robert McKimson, writer Warren Foster, and Selzer's successor, John Burton. Photograph property of Warner Bros.

Warner Bros., in 1955, was the first major studio to embrace network television production, and they established a very close relationship with ABC. By 1960, with the studio's earlier cartoons showing success in syndication, it was time for Warner's animated stars to make a run at the new medium. For "The Bugs Bunny Show" an ingenious format was devised that combined new animation with old to create an inexpensive yet entertaining weekly half hour. The prime-time entry featured Bugs as host—frequently interacting with the jealous Daffy and other characters in the WB stable. The host segments were newly created and often maintained a storyline that carried through the entire show. The old cartoons that were inserted into the program were, in effect, sketches, and the result was the animated equivalent of "The Jackie Gleason Show" (McKimson, in fact, directed a delightful send-up of Gleason and company in "The Honey-Mousers" [1956]), and other then-popular programs. Jones, Freleng, and McKimson collaborated closely for the first time in their Warner careers, and even the commercials often featured the show's stars. The series provided many with a "night of nights"—complete with high ratings—as its opening theme promised, until 1962 (when it moved to Saturday morning). Having set a remarkable precedent for the studio's future TV outings, Bugs and friends have been on the air in one form or another, without interruption, ever since!

Unfortunately, "The Bugs Bunny Show" proved one of the original Warner cartoon studio's last hurrahs. Show business economics, at the time dictated by the divorce of the large studios from their theater chains and the arrival of television, all but eliminated the short subject from the movie theater's program. Cartoons were no longer, in theatrical terms, sufficiently profitable to justify their expense. As a result, beginning in the 1950s, the major studios began the slow but inexorable process of shutting down their cartoon production.

George Burns, Mel Blanc, and Gracie Allen, early 1940s. Photograph property of Warner Bros.

Warner, however, had a relationship with ABC that made television a practical new venue for its animated output. Indeed, in addition to "The Bugs Bunny Show," Warner had produced, in 1962, a Chuck Jones "Road Runner" pilot *The Adventures of the Road Runner* (which featured a talking, "super genius" version of the Coyote), and in 1963 a Friz Freleng pilot called "Philbert" (a situation comedy that combined live action and animation). But Warner's special relationship with ABC was coming to an end, and these projects never reached fruition. Instead, in 1963, in-house cartoon production at Warner Bros. ceased. Jones and Freleng left to pursue other opportunities while McKimson remained to direct segments of the Don Knotts feature, *The Incredible Mr. Limpett*. With the completion of that feature, Warner ended thirty-three years of continuous animation production.

Enough cartoons had been produced before the shutdown, however, to release into 1964. And sometime before the release of that last cartoon, *Senorella and the Glass Huarache*, Warner Bros. had a change of heart. They wanted new cartoons but no longer maintained a staff with which to produce them. Fortunately, Friz Freleng had recently started his own company, so Warner offered Freleng and his partner, David DePatie, the opportunity to produce cartoons featuring their old Looney Tunes characters. Thus, DePatie-Freleng Enterprises created new shorts for Warner Bros. over the next three years.

The DePatie-Freleng cartoons primarily starred either the newly antagonistic team of Speedy Gonzales and Daffy Duck, or the popular Road Runner and Coyote (the bulk of which were directed by a veteran of Chuck Jones's unit, Rudy Larriva, as well as Bob McKimson and Hawley Pratt). Warner continued a regular program of animated theatrical releases and even introduced a Saturday morning "Road

The House That Jack Built: The main entrance to Warner Bros. studios, c. 1960. Photograph property of Warner Bros.

Runner Show" featuring old cartoons with some new segments produced by DePatie and Freleng. In 1967, they decided to return to in-house production.

The studio hired producer Bill Hendricks to augment the existing stock company of Warner cartoon stars with newer, more contemporary creations. Enter Cool Cat, Merlin the Magic Mouse, and Bunny and Claude. With voices provided by comedian Larry Storch, there was a genuine attempt to inject something new into the Warner cartoon mix. The results were uneven, to say the least, but perhaps it's fair to comment that these new-fangled characters were hardly given a proper chance to prove themselves because in 1969, *Injun Trouble* heralded a long pause in Warner cartoon short subject production after thirty-nine years of continuous activity. It was directed by a man all too familiar with the shift in fortune of the studio—the venerable Robert McKimson who had been with the animation department almost from its beginning.

The Saturday morning network shows continued with phenomenal ratings, the old cartoons were also regularly seen on local stations, and the characters were known to pop up in newly produced television commercials. But production of new theatrical cartoon shorts was nil.

It's hard to keep a good rabbit (or chicken hawk) down. Renewed interest in the classic Warner's cartoons, fueled by scattered festivals on college campuses, arthouse movie theaters, and grassroots neighborhood cinemas, led to a plethora of writings in scholarly journals, as the Hollywood Cartoon was finally given its due as an authentic American art form. Tributes to Warner Animation by no less than the Academy of Motion Picture Arts and Sciences and other celebrated institutions of the arts followed. And in 1976, Chuck Jones, responding to the public's crying need for new Warner films done in the Golden Age animation style of yore, produced a brand new prime-time special, featuring that ever-contentious duo, Bugs Bunny and Daffy Duck. Assisted by conductor Michael Tilson-Thomas, Bugs and Daffy performed the orchestral "Carnival of the Animals." The special was a huge success, and CBS began ordering new specials from Warner, beginning a series of highly rated prime-time events that continued well into the 1980s. Hal Geer, Warner Bros. Cartoons vice-president, produced many of the new projects which, like "The Bugs Bunny Show," combined new animation and old into half-hours unified by a continuing story or theme.

The 1979 holiday season was ushered in by "Bugs Bunny's Looney Christmas Tales," the first of a number of television specials featuring all-new shorts directed by Chuck Jones and Friz Freleng. That same year, Jones directed the first in a new series of Warner compilation features for theatrical release. Bugs and the Road Runner teamed up in *The Bugs Bunny-Road Runner Movie*, which brought the precocious pair to the prestigious New York Film Festival. And a new Merrie Melodies

OF ALL THE JUICE JOINTS. Limited Edition. Warner Bros. Classic Animation, 1996. With a classic 1940s "feel" and a reverence for Looney Tunes past, *Carrotblanca* invites you to join the fez-tivities at "Café au Lait American." The short paid homage to the classic Warner Bros. film, *Casablanca*.

cartoon—a Duck Dodgers sequel—was not far behind, the first Merrie Melodies produced in some ten years.

In response to the success of Chuck Jones's compiled filmography, Friz Freleng returned to production. Freleng's *Looney, Looney, Looney Bugs Bunny Movie* was just the first of three major compilation features he produced in his effort to reengage the studio in animation production.

The climax to Warner's amazing cartoon renaissance was probably the massive film retrospective and art show mounted at New York's Museum of Modern Art, which received nationwide attention. Friz Freleng said of this black-tie museum affair: "That was one of the biggest events of that kind I've ever gone to. Even winning the Academy Awards didn't feel like that. Here it was just Chuck and me, and everyone was congratulating us. We got all the attention. That's the first time it had ever happened to either one of us, I suppose." By the early 1990s, Freleng and Jones both had stars on Hollywood's Walk of Fame, an unspoken statement on how highly regarded animation had become as an art form.

Freleng again left the studio in the mid-1980s, but by then the animation studio's revival was in full swing. Television specials starring the classic characters were having great ratings success, and the feature film compilations were drawing in yet another generation of fans. The studio began to find a new direction away from short subjects and toward expanding new technology in filmmaking. Additionally invigorating the studio was the 1988 compilation feature *Daffy Duck's Quackbusters*. Warner by then had regained enough momentum to entrust production of two new shorts to a whole new generation of young artists whose devotion to the art matched that of the early pioneers. Co-producers Steven S. Greene and Kathleen Helppie-Shipley brought on Greg Ford and Terry Lennon to direct the new cartoons, the well-received spoofs *Night of the Living Duck* and *The Duxorcist* (the directing team went on to create several "compilation specials" and new shorts for television).

The year 1988 surely marked an important turning point for Warner Bros. Classic Animation, WB characters joining a host of other animated stars in the Disney/Steven Spielberg feature *Who Framed Roger Rabbit*, a remarkably complicated technological *tour de force* that literally shoved audiences into the world of the "Toons." The studio was poised to take its next step forward in animation.

With the enormous success of *Roger Rabbit*, Spielberg was eager to continue exploring his love affair with cartoons, particularly those from the Warner Bros. studio. Warner was more than happy to join with this young cinematic genius, calling upon the talents of producer/writer Tom Ruegger and executive producer Jean MacCurdy to pull together a creative team for the challenge. MacCurdy, Ruegger, and Spielberg collaborated to create the TV series "Tiny Toon Adventures," which

MASTERS OF ANIMATION. Limited Edition. Warner Bros Classic Animation, 1996. The studio pays tribute to the magnificent seven who made Warner cartoons what they are today, surrounded by the Looney Tunes characters.

TWAPPED. Signed Limited Edition. Friz Freleng, 1983. Twapped? Hardly. Forget the sweet little look on the canary's face; director Freleng won his first Oscar playing off of Tweety's somewhat less-than-passive personality, even in the face of a bad ol' puddy tat.

premiered in 1990 and founded the new subdivision called Warner Bros. Television Animation.

The TV unit's output, some with Spielberg, some independent of him, has been prolific under MacCurdy and Ruegger, whose award-winning production credits so far include "Tiny Toon Adventures," "Taz-Mania," "Animaniacs," "Batman: The Animated Series," "Pinky and The Brain," "The Sylvester and Tweety Mysteries," "Freakazoid," "Road Rovers," and "Superman"—enough quality cartoon time to keep any Saturday morning viewer happily glued to the tube.

In 1990, the Classic Animation studio (with executive producer Kathleen Helppie-Shipley in charge) celebrated Bugs Bunny's fiftieth birthday by starring the veteran of screen and TV in a brand new theatrical cartoon, *Box Office Bunny*, directed by Darrell Van Citters. The production of theatrical shorts continued with such recent entries as *Carrotblanca* (directed by Douglas McCarthy) and Chuck Jones Studio's own *Superior Duck* (under the Warner Bros. aegis). Jones even produced a new Road Runner cartoon (*Chariots of Fur*) and a long-awaited sequel to his original Michigan J. Frog cartoon, this one entitled *Another Froggy Evening*.

Classic Animation's prolific and award-winning commercial team has brought Bugs Bunny to the Academy Awards show to deliver Oscars on three separate occasions (once with Daffy), and created innovative and entertaining television spots with the characters (often interacting with live-action stars such as Deion Sanders and super-athlete Michael

87/252

Jordan)—short masterpieces that have won major advertising, animation, and film awards for their creative prowess.

And so, the Looney Tunes legacy continues. Today members of the Warner Bros. menagerie star in every modern motion picture format: from theatrical feature films, commercials, psa's, and TV series to CD Roms, video games, and screen savers. As the media evolve (with the advent of CGI and a refined, impeccable form of 3-D animation), so do the Warner animated characters, in the hands of a new generation of artists, producers, directors, and writers, whose creative energies keep the legacy alive. To paraphrase Bugs Bunny (and one of his most illustrious mentors, Groucho Marx)—"Of course, you know this means *more!*"

AIR AND HARE. Limited Edition. Warner Bros. Classic Animation, 1992. Michael Jordan teaches Bugs how to dribble. And Bugs teaches Michael how to handle bullies in this cel based on their first commercial together. This inspired (and technically astounding) pairing led to the feature film *Space Jam*.

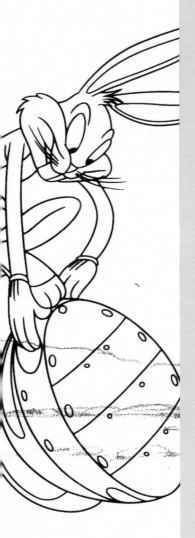

TEX AVERY

BOB CLAMPETT

FRIZ FRELENG

CHUCK JONES

ROBERT McKIMSON

ADDITIONAL DIRECTORS

ADDITIONAL ARTISTS

MUSIC AND SOUND

THE CREATORS

Tex Avery

Fred "Tex" Avery, for his short tenure at the studio, could still be considered one of the "fathers" of the Warner Bros. cartoon style, since it was his zany "take" on animated cartooning that became the studio's signature. Starting as a Walter Lantz animator in the early 1930s, Avery longed to improve what he saw as run-of-the-mill cartoons and finally got his chance in 1935 when Leon Schlesinger needed a director for a third cartoon unit he was creating.

Avery's Porky Pig unit at "Termite Terrace" broke the mold for humor, story, and pacing in animated cartoons. He resisted the move toward realism that was overtaking the other Hollywood cartoon studios and made impossible situations, exaggerated facial expressions, and popular slang trademarks of his work. Avery's sense of humor attracted some of the most creative young talents at the studio (particularly Chuck Jones and Bob Clampett), and together they did something revolutionary —they made cartoons to entertain themselves, and in the process entertained an ever-larger audience. Suddenly, slow-paced cartoons about flower pageants and lost bear cubs were supplanted by wild cartoons about mad bombers, rain-making pills, and wacky wrestling matches. Avery and his animators helped put the rise in Porky's star, created Daffy Duck, and, in 1940, directed the first Bugs Bunny cartoon, *A Wild Hare*.

The best Avery cartoons parodied movie genres like gangster pictures (*Thugs With Dirty Mugs*, 1939), fairy tales (*Cinderella Meets Fella*, 1938), and Busby Berkeley musicals (*Miss Glory*, a.k.a. *Page Miss Glory* 1936). By the 1940s he had begun to lampoon even the conventions of filmmaking with gags concerning split screens (*Cross Country Detours*, 1940), movie credits (*Tortoise Beats Hare*, 1941), and animation itself (the unique stick-figure cartoons in *Porky's Preview*, 1941). He also pioneered the spoof newsreel/travelogue and broke the "fourth wall" by having characters speak directly to the audience, thus establishing a conspiratorial tone that would become a hallmark of Warner Bros. Cartoons.

A brash, defiant humor was the key to Warner Bros.' dominance in cartoon short subjects, and Tex Avery set the standard. But when Leon Schlesinger deleted the (now-lost) gag ending to 1942's *The Heckling Hare*, the headstrong Avery moved over to MGM where he continued making great cartoons for more than a decade. However, he never again worked with characters with the lasting appeal of Bugs Bunny, Daffy Duck, and Porky Pig—his legacy to Warners and the foundation of their cartoon empire.

THE HECKLING HARE. Limited Edition. Warner Bros./Tex Avery, 1993. In the released version of *The Heckling Hare* (1942), the dog (and Bugs) survive the fall and land safely on the ground—while Avery, after an argument over the edit, landed at MGM.

(*Previous spread*) THE PROCESS OF ANIMATION. Limited Edition. Bob Clampett, 1996. From rough sketch to clean-up to ink and paint, the process is brought to life in this limited-edition pan-cel.

DAFFY DUCK IN HOLLYWOOD. Limited Edition. Warner Bros./Tex Avery, 1994. Daffy Duck's persistent recutting of Avery's meticulously timed sequences infuriated the director in *Daffy Duck In Hollywood* (1938).

A WILD HARE. Limited Edition. Virgil Ross, 1993. "What's up, Doc?" Avery's *A Wild Hare* (1940) was the start of the now-familiar Bugs/Elmer relationship.

Bob Clampett

O ne of the most brilliantly bizarre minds ever to work not only in animation but in all of film, Bob Clampett could handily be called "the man who put the 'Looney' in Looney Tunes."

Born in San Diego, California, in 1913, Clampett's childhood was populated with the families of movie industry workers and occasional actors, and he grew up with a keen interest in theater and its brother arts: puppetry, music, cartooning, and filmmaking. At twelve, Clampett was directing his own short subjects, and within a few years he was making his own amateur films. In 1930, Leon Schlesinger, impressed with Clampett when the budding filmmaker had brought one of his 16mm shorts to Schlesinger's company for titling, offered him a job at the new Harman-Ising Studio.

Within a few months, Clampett had stuck his fingers into every pie in the studio. Officially an assistant animator, he hung around the story department more than a little, and when Schlesinger took over the studio, received a promotion to full animator status. There he modified Porky's design, making him slimmer and cuter, while his characters and cartoons grew more wildly unpredictable and frenetic.

Bob Clampett's animation squashed, pulled, stretched, shook, shimmied, bounced, and rattled the Looney Tunes characters, as if their spirits were trying to break free from the impediment of a body. Taking the spirit of Tex Avery to another level, the director's approach to his cartoons left an indelible (and frenetic) mark on what is now regarded as the "Warner Bros. animation style."

(*Left*) WELCOME TO WACKYLAND. Limited Edition. Bob Clampett, 1991. It Can Happen Here: *Porky in Wackyland* (1938) is one of Clampett's best.

(*Opposite, top*) SLINGSHOT SHIELD. Limited Edition. Bob Clampett, 1991. The Do-Do (seemingly with studio approval) attempts to render Porky extinct in this scene from the Clampett classic *Porky in Wackyland* (1938).

(*Opposite, below*) A CORNY CONCERTO. Limited Edition. Bob Clampett, 1992. Bob Clampett's A Corny Concerto (1943), with a story by Frank Tashlin, is a brilliant spoof of Disney's *Fantasia*.

As a junior "supervisor," Clampett worked in Schlesinger's equivalent of the minor leagues, the black-and-white Looney Tunes which starred Porky Pig (as oppposed to the then more prestigious Technicolor Merrie Melodies cartoons). They were his college education, each with a unique charm all its own that together served as valuable building blocks toward his mature style. Clampett, beginning to master the quicksilver tempos and the tone of raucous insanity brought to animation by his "hero," Tex Avery, began by responding to the "cute" cartoon tradition prevalent in the late 1930s as fallout from Disney. But even when Clampett's characters stand around looking cuddly (as they often do) in his black-and-white years, he takes what might be considered heavy-handed and filters it through the sensibilities of a true anarchist.

This quality would blossom in his color cartoons of the mid-1940s, which by any standard include many of the funniest moments in the history of animated film. Clampett, who loved rounded cuteness and "stretch-and-squash" animation in equal proportions, juxtaposed the two in remarkable ways. The bumbling gentility of Elmer Fudd is hilariously repulsive in *Wabbit Twouble* (1941), and Daffy Duck, in *The Wise Quacking Duck* (1943), and Bugs Bunny, in *The Wacky Wabbit* (1942), are endowed with a positively irresistible charm that shines through even their most hostile behavior. And then there's Tweety, designed after the director's own baby pictures. In Clampett's *Birdy And The Beast* (1944), the canary's sometimes shocking use of self-defensive violence was made hilarious by his babylike cuteness.

(*Top*) MY HERO. Limited Edition. Bob Clampett, 1994. Bugs Bunny returns the idiotic Beaky Buzzard to his mother in this image, inspired by Bob Clampett's *Bugs Bunny Gets The Boid*.

(*Above*) THE BIG SNOOZE. Limited Edition. Bob Clampett, 1993. Clampett's *The Big Snooze* (1946) is anything but. This scene is from the bizarre dream sequence that takes up three quarters of the picture.

(*Left*) ANY BONDS TODAY? Limited Edition. Bob Clampett, 1990. A scene from *Any Bonds Today?*, a trailer urging audiences to buy war bonds and stamps that was rushed into theaters in early 1942.

(*Opposite*) WABBIT TWOUBLE (TITLE) Limited Edition. Bob Clampett, 1992. This piece and the two following were sold as part of a series of title card limited editions.

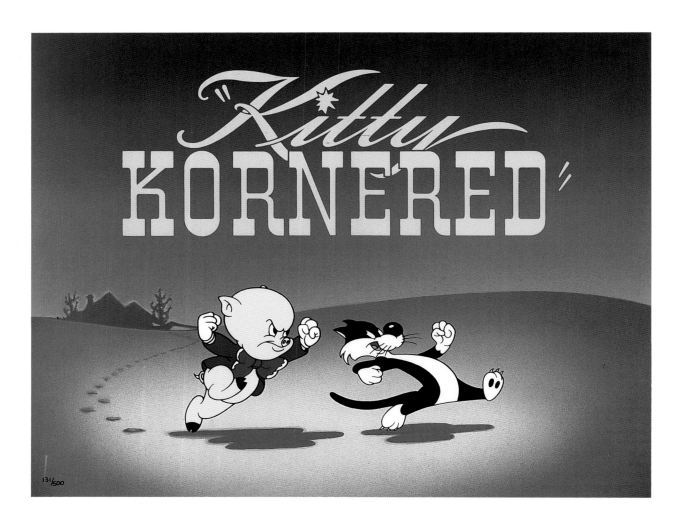

(Left) KITTY KORNERED (TITLE).
Limited Edition. Bob Clampett,
1992.

(Opposite) BIRDY AND THE
BEAST. Limited Edition. Bob
Clampett, 1992.

Apart from these *tours de force* of character direction, Clampett also came out with any number of remarkable one-shot epics. His Disney parodies *Coal Black and de Sebben Dwarfs* (1943) and *A Corny Concerto* (1943), his homages to Hollywood personalities in *Bacall to Arms* (1946), *A Tale of Two Kitties* (1942), and *A Gruesome Twosome* (1945), and his accurate send-up of the Academy Awards in *What's Cookin' Doc?* (1944) bespeak Clampett's adoration of Hollywood at the same time he lampoons it. Lastly, there are Clampett films along the lines of *The Big Snooze* (1946), *Book Revue* (1946), and *Tin Pan Alley Cats* (1943) that can only be described as reels of pure, undiluted wackiness.

Clampett left Warner Bros. at the peak of his creative powers, leaving to speculation how the characters might have grown had he stayed. His most celebrated post-Warner ventures were a pair of TV programs, the first a televised-live puppet program called "Time for Beany" that ran from 1949 to 1957 (which made Clampett a television superstar), and the animated version of the show, "Beany and Cecil," produced in 1961.

(*Above*) BUGS MIRANDA. Limited Edition. Bob Clampett, 1996. The award–winning rabbit in a scene from Clampett's Oscar ceremony spoof *What's Cookin' Doc?* After being pelted with fruit by the members of the Academy, Bugs emerges à la Carmen Miranda, one of the funniest gags in the picture.

(*Below*) DAFFY MODEL SHEET. Limited Edition. Bob Clampett, 1994. Daffy Duck, Clampett style.

(*Opposite*) BUGS PERSONA. Limited Edition. Bob Clampett, 1994. Under Bob Clampett's direction, Bugs Bunny was truly a "Rabbit of a Thousand Faces." Clockwise from top left, the first two pencil poses are from *What's Cookin' Doc?* (1944), the rest from *A Corny Concerto* (1943), *The Old Grey Hare* (1944), *Hare Ribbin'* (1944), and *Any Bonds Today?* (1942).

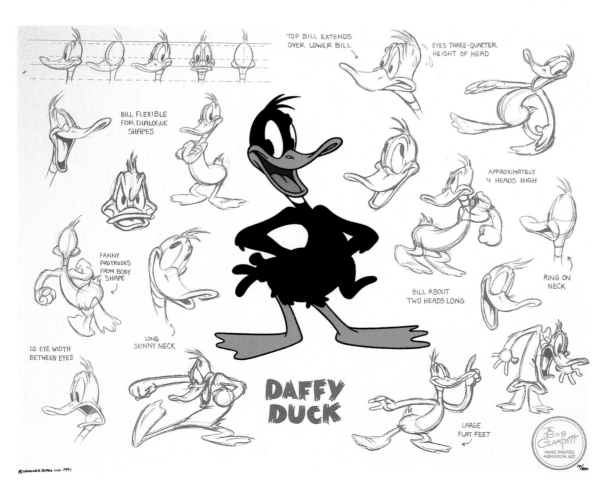

BC1018

Friz Freleng

Friz Freleng (seated) and his key layout artist, Hawley Pratt, c. 1960. Photograph property of Warner Bros.

Whenever cartoon professionals and animation historians are asked to rank the medium's all-time greatest directors in some sort of hierarchy, the name Friz Freleng is always placed among those on the topmost tier. Yet the "Friz Freleng style" has proved exceedingly difficult to codify in a single, simple catchphrase that does full justice to his staggering range. While it's true that many individual films directed by Freleng have received a great deal of critical attention over the years (the Oscar-winners *Tweetie Pie*, *Speedy Gonzales*, *Birds Anonymous*, and *Knighty Knight Bugs*; perennial cult favorites such as *Little Red Riding Rabbit*, *Rhapsody Rabbit*, and *Canned Feud*), it is possible that Friz himself has never been given his due. The explanation is simple: Freleng's prolific output isn't so much overlooked as simply taken for granted as being virtually synonymous with Warner Bros. Animation at large. Freleng was a true *sine qua non* of the animation department, his work and the studio's work mutually reflective. Simply put, without Freleng there would be no Warner Bros. cartoon "style."

Take the 1930s. Even by mid-decade, Friz had been around a little longer than anybody else, having started with Disney in the mid-1920s on the *Oswald The Lucky Rabbit* series and having served as the key animator

Leon Schlesinger and Porky Pig in a still from Freleng's short, *You Ought To Be In Pictures*. Photograph property of Warner Bros. Colorized version.

WATCH ME PASTE THIS PATHETIC PALOOKA WITH A POWERFUL PARALYZING PERFECT PACHYDERMAS PERCUSSION PITCH!

PALOOKA PITCH. Signed Limited Edition. Friz Freleng, 1995. Long before Bugs Bunny discovered basketball, *Baseball Bugs* (1946) pitted our Rabbit against the Gas-House Gorillas.

BASEBALL BUGS. Signed Limited Edition. Friz Freleng,
1990. Freleng's Bugs was always a tough competitor but a
good sport.

on the very first cartoon released by Warner, *Sinkin' In the Bathtub* (1930). Soon promoted to senior director (most of Warner's later personnel first apprenticed under Friz), Freleng influenced the early Merrie Melodies, little mini-musicals the covert purpose of which was to plug Warner-copyrighted pop songs. And one might say that he made some of the studio's most identity-defining (and Academy Award–showered) films of the 1940s and 1950s. Freleng launched the careers of Porky Pig and Sylvester the Cat (not to mention lesser luminaries such as the gangsters "Rocky and Mugsy," and Tweety's dotty protectress, Granny) along the way.

A "genre" director *par excellence*, Freleng had an extraordinary ability to incorporate and synthesize studio-favored trends of a particular era, yet still create what one would consider fully self-contained, even personal, work. Every ardent animation fan is familiar with the 1940 docu-cartoon *You Ought To Be In Pictures*, in which Porky first leaves and then shamefacedly returns to the studio, welcomed back into the fold by Leon Schlesinger. Fewer are familiar with the semi-autobiographical connection it has to its director: by Freleng's daughter Hope's account, the film, in fact, was made as a roundabout apology to Schlesinger for a brief year-and-a-half stint at MGM. And—talk about autobiographical— few casual viewers would ever know that the very personality of that little fireball rabbit-hater Yosemite Sam, unveiled by Freleng in *Hare Trigger*, was based on the personality of Friz himself. Yosemite Sam, down to his pint-sized stature and notoriously short-fused temper, was Friz's very funny, very self-deprecatory self-portrait, serving at the same time as an ideal nemesis for Bugs, the studio's biggest star.

Freleng dealt with the ever-changing canvas of "genre" cartooning over the years: from the often charming Merrie Melodies and other early-1930s fare, to the more expressive "screwball school" of the 1940s, with its development of such stars as Bugs Bunny and Daffy Duck, and the more self-consciously design-heavy stylization of the 1950s. During all of this, Friz qualified as an active participant in the absolute center of cartoon production at Warner. Freleng willingly made use of these different waves of influence, reformulating them to create cartoons that made sense (and were actually funny!) on their own terms. Friz was always a man of his time, responding to trends but never riding them, always staying in his own distinctive lane. He could assimilate the considerable changes in animation over the years (especially the revolutionary look of UPA) and each time around make them uniquely his own, broadly applying certain favorite techniques of music-synchronization, a unique staging of action (including a consistently inventive use of off-screen space), and, especially in Friz's case, comic timing.

Freleng's musical aplomb, of course, is well-documented, and the trademark dance numbers that often spontaneously erupt in his cartoons

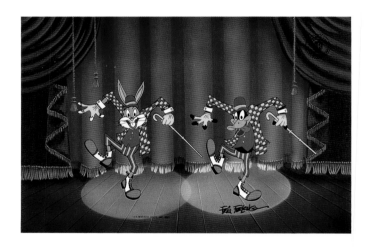

(*Top*) BIG HOUSE BUNNY. Limited Edition. Warner Bros. Classic Animation, 1990. When you're Bugs Bunny (directed by Freleng), iron bars do not a prison make, although Yosemite Sam doesn't believe it until the tables are turned on him.

(*Above*) THE ENTERTAINERS. Signed Limited Edition. Friz Freleng, 1991. Despite their adversarial relationship, Bugs and Daffy are hoofers at heart.

RHAPSODY RABBIT. Signed Limited Edition. Friz Freleng,
1991. Freleng's use of music and dance was unsurpassed in
the field. This cel, inspired by *Rhapsody Rabbit* (1946), offers
up some of the "cool" Bugs was known for.

are always welcome treats. His pioneering burlesques of classical music, *Rhapsody in Rivets* and *Pigs in a Polka*, formally introduced the stylistic notion of *over*-synchronization (as opposed to Disney's *Fantasia*'s more straightforwardly lyrical approach), so that construction workers have to scurry like crazy to erect a skyscraper to the strains of Franz Liszt, and the Three Little Pigs perform a lurch-tempoed ballet set to Johannes Brahms. These two justifiably famous films were highly influential, both within Warners and industry-wide, but to mistakenly typecast Freleng as just a maker of musicals is to miss the fact that he applied the same utterly marvelous manipulation of rhythm in *all* his cartoons: the meticulously metered "Pick up pie!" slapstick of *Slick Hare*, pitcher Bugs's lightning "fast ball" followed by his agonizingly slow one in *Baseball Bugs*, Yosemite Sam's repeated climbs and fateful falls in *High-Diving Hare*, and Sylvester's stealthy and methodical tiptoeing and stacking up of bric-a-brac to reach Tweety's cage in numerous pictures. While Chuck Jones praises his colleague as having "the most magnificent timing sense of any man I've known," Freleng's genius was his canny ability to unselfconsciously inject his talents into the comedy so all that showed was the laughter.

(*Above*) WHO DONE IT? Signed Limited Edition. Friz Freleng, 1990. Framed? Only Sylvester knows for sure, but the shadow on the wall says he won't have time to explain.

(*Below*) BAD PUDDY TAT. Signed Limited Edition. Friz Freleng, 1987. Inspired by a gag in the Oscar-winning *Tweetie Pie* (1947), Sylvester is the cat that will *never* swallow the canary.

THE SHOWDOWN. Signed Limited Edition. Friz Freleng,
1994. Two of Bugs Bunny's greatest foes (and two of Mel
Blanc's most difficult voices) face off in this special scene
created for the collectors' market.

Chuck Jones

harles M. "Chuck" Jones is to many people the definitive Warner cartoon director. His best shorts are the result of a kind of sublime tension between the seeming contradictions he represents. He is a master both of pure graphics and the realistic rendering of subtle emotions. His cartoons can be as wild as an untamed bronco, yet as locked into rules and regulations as an evening of Japanese Kabuki. He spans the history of the Warner Bros. cartoon, from the 1930s to the eve of the next millennium, still creating and still directing.

Chuck Jones started out washing used animation cels at the Ub Iwerks studio, but made it to Warner Bros. just in time to animate alongside young Bob Clampett in the new Tex Avery unit at ramshackle "Termite Terrace." Quickly distinguishing himself, he became a director whose early cartoons reflected his fascination with small details, both emotional and physical. Viewing early Jones characters, such as his first

66/500

©1993 Warner Bros.

Ain't I A Stinker? Signed Limited Edition. Chuck Jones, 1993. In a word, yes. Another great moment for Bugs Bunny as he plays animator and torments Daffy Duck in this final shot of *Duck Amuck* (1953).

star creation, Sniffles, is like looking into the sketch books of an extremely talented art student. Countless experiments in character expression were to pay off a thousand fold when ultimately grafted upon the likes of Bugs Bunny, Daffy Duck, and Wile E. Coyote ("super genius").

Jones's collaboration with gagman Michael Maltese from the late 1940s into the 1960s resulted in a maniacal mixture of wildness and minutiae that changed the course of everything it touched. Their Bugs Bunny/Daffy Duck comedies such as *Rabbit Seasoning* and *Duck! Rabbit, Duck!* established a relationship so vivid that the mere sight of the characters together in the opening of the later "Bugs Bunny Show" spoke volumes about the deliciously devilish essence of competition. Jones's diagnosis of Daffy as neurotic rather than "crazy" made such interaction possible. And the detailed definition of his Road Runner and Coyote—and their necessarily and (to say the least) intense—relationship made even their wildest gags believable.

As Jones's unit entered its most fertile period, the 1950s, a smoothly operating team was in place that included background artist Philip DeGuard, production designer Maurice Noble, and noted animators Ken Harris, Ben Washam, and Abe Levitow. Together they

(Above) PEWLITZER PRIZE. Signed Limited Edition. Chuck Jones, 1993. The award will probably go to the "scent"-imental favorite.

(Below) SOUNDSTAGE. Signed Limited Edition. Chuck Jones, 1991.

CHARIOTS OF FUR (TITLE). Signed Limited Edition. Chuck Jones, 1995. Jones's most recent Road Runner and Coyote epic continues the classic chase to the end of the millennium and then some.

were able to realize Jones's most creative ambitions and produced such abiding classics as *Duck Dodgers in the 24 1/2th Century, What's Opera, Doc?*, and *Rabbit of Seville*. He also created an array of beloved Warner Bros. characters including Marvin The Martian, Pepé Le Pew, and the aforementioned Road Runner, plus such memorable minor characters as Hubie and Bertie, Ralph Phillips, and Charlie Dog.

In the 1960s, Jones's interests shifted. With the closing of the original Warner animation studio, he moved on to long-form projects—including TV adaptations of Dr. Seuss's *How the Grinch Stole Christmas*, Walt Kelly's *Pogo*, and a feature-length theatrical, *The Phantom Tollbooth*. However, he remained true to Bugs, Daffy, and his other cartoon colleagues and in 1976 produced a TV adaptation of the musical composition *Carnival of the Animals* featuring his favorite rabbit and duck. That special inaugurated a new round of Warner cartoon production which continues to this day.

(*Above*) PLANET X. Signed Limited Edition. Chuck Jones, 1994. Daffy "Duck Dodgers" encounters peevish Marvin The Martian in a losing battle, based on the 1953 Jones short *Duck Dodgers in the 24 1/2th Century*.

(*Below*) RABBIT OF SEVILLE (IV). Signed Limited Edition. Chuck Jones, 1994. The rascally Rabbit is about to start a "Seville" war. *Rabbit of Seville* (1950) is a robust chase around the opera stage that incorporates traditional Bugs Bunny gags into a classical music setting—with spectacular results.

(*Opposite, top*) TRUANT OFFICER. Signed Limited Edition. Chuck Jones, 1994. Jones redraws a classic confrontation from *Bewitched Bunny* (1954), featuring Witch Hazel and Hansel and Gretel.

(*Opposite, bottom*) THE FANATIC. Signed Limited Edition. Chuck Jones, 1991. The famous George Santayana quote, made eminently clear in this limited-edition cel inspired by Jones's own series of Road Runner/Wile E. Coyote shorts.

For reducing even the most stalwart of viewers to giggles, Jones has received some of the industry's most prestigious honors. He has been fêted by the Museum of the Moving Image in London and Hollywood's own Academy of Motion Picture Arts and Sciences, from whom he received a lifetime-achievement Oscar in 1996. *What's Opera, Doc?* is the first animated short-subject to be inducted into the National Film Registry. And a list of the fifty greatest cartoons of all time, compiled by animation creators, has Jones in five of the top ten positions. Not bad for a man who has said he secretly relates to Daffy Duck.

(Below) ROCKET SQUAD. Signed Limited Edition. Chuck Jones, 1994. 50% sci-fi parody, 50% cop-show spoof =100% funny. Chuck Jones's *Rocket Squad* (1956) is not a sequel to *Duck Dodgers*, but a clever spoof of *Dragnet*.

(Opposite) Jones reinvented Daffy Duck as an egotisticial, neurotic foil during the 1950s. (Top, left) 18TH HARE. Signed Limited Edition. Chuck Jones, 1993. The Duck faces frustration at never being able to play through on Bugs's turf. (Middle, left) SHAKE HANDS WITH FRIAR DUCK. Signed Limited Edition. Chuck Jones, 1988. Daffy reluctantly accepts his fate in this final gag from *Robin Hood Daffy* (1958). (Bottom, left) FISH TALE. Signed Limited Edition. Chuck Jones, 1995. Warners' characters take on human traits to such an extent we forget that Daffy is a water fowl, not a fisherman. (Right) DUCK DODGERS FINALE. Signed Limited Edition. Chuck Jones, 1993. Daffy rejoices in the final, hollow victory at the climax of *Duck Dodgers in the 24 1/2th Century* (1953).

50/500   *Chuck Jones*
© 1994 *Warner Bros.*

Robert McKimson

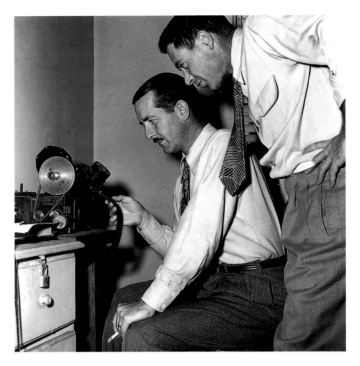

obert McKimson, whose stint at Warner Bros. went uninterrupted from 1933 until 1969, is regarded among animation fans as the consummate professional of the Warner directors, his workmanlike efforts solid and serviceable. And in his early years—particularly the 1940s—McKimson also evidenced a flair for comedy that more than justified his position as one of the studio's star directors. While often overshadowed by Jones's groundbreaking stylistic reputation and Freleng's magical musicality, the twice Oscar-nominated McKimson's funniest cartoons are joyously full of inspired silliness and Warner Bros.' animation anarchy (witness Bugs's decimation of Nero the Lion in *Acrobatty Bunny*, or the hideous glee of the Three Little Pigs in *The Windblown Hare* that makes audiences sympathize with the wolf).

When the studio promoted McKimson to director status—beginning with 1946's *Daffy Doodles*—it was an acknowledgment of the vital contribution this remarkable draftsman had already made to the art as designer and animator. (Both of McKimson's brothers, Tom and Charles, were animators at Warner Bros.). Thanks to the series of widely used model sheets McKimson drew in the 1940s, he can be credited with

(Above) Robert McKimson (seated) and one of his animators, Rod Scribner, review a piece of animation test film on a movieola machine. Photograph property of Warner Bros.

(Below) HOW MANY LUMPS? Limited Edition. Robert McKimson, 1993. This is a great set-up from *Rabbit's Kin* (1952), featuring Pete Puma's memorable first appearance.

(Opposite) VINTAGE BUGS. Limited Edition. Robert McKimson (facsimile signature), 1991. McKimson drew this classic image of Bugs Bunny, Warners' greatest star.

AP 1/15

Robert McKimson

creating the definitive look of the characters in the Looney Tunes stable. Then too, as an animator, he was party to the effectiveness of key sequences in many of the Bob Clampett classics of the mid-1940s. In his art he was fast, he was fluid, and he was on-the-money.

Clampett praised McKimson as a colossal animator who should have continued animating, even though the offer to direct was irresistible. Still, McKimson's first dozen or so classic Bugs Bunny episodes—including *Easter Yeggs* (1947) and *Gorilla My Dreams* (1948)—take a back seat to no one's. His 1940s efforts—particularly the early Foghorn Leghorn films (one of which, *Walky Talky Hawky*, was nominated for an Oscar)— benefit keenly from the ace humor of writer Warren Foster. And it was McKimson thinking out loud with writer Sid Marcus that led to the incomparable Tasmanian Devil, whose five cartoons were among J. L. Warner's own favorites.

(*Top*) GORILLA MY DREAMS. Limited Edition. Robert McKimson, 1993. Inspired by the McKimson cartoon, this scene shows Bugs's joy, short-lived as it is, at being adopted by Mr. and Mrs. Gruesome Gorilla.

(*Above*) HOLLYWOOD HARE. Limited Edition. Robert McKimson (facsimile signature), 1991. "What's Up, Doc?" is the question *and* the McKimson cartoon inspiration for this image, which plays up Bugs's celebrity as he eagerly relates his life story to Disassociated Press.

(*Left*) BUGS AND HONEY. Limited Edition. Robert McKimson (facsimile signature), 1993. Though she has never appeared in animated cartoons, Bugs Bunny's girlfriend Honey Bunny was popular in merchandising and in comic books. Robert McKimson designed her for licensing in the late 1950s and she is still in use today.

HILLBILLY HARE. Limited Edition. Robert McKimson, 1994. One of McKimson's best, *Hillbilly Hare* (1950) features an extended square dance sequence loaded with gags. As the dance caller, Bugs tricks the two mountain men into pulling their beards, wallowing in a pig pen, and getting bundled in a hay baler—among other indignities.

Additional Directors

One of the secrets to Warner Bros.' dominance of the short theatrical cartoon was its unusual breadth of directorial talent. Most studios would have been grateful to have had one director of Chuck Jones's or Friz Freleng's caliber on their roster, but Warners possessed a wealth of directorial greats.

Arthur Davis, whose career began during the silent era, was one such talent. Though he was a top Warner animator both before and after his directorial stint, his brief late 1940s tenure deserves special note. He introduced the Goofy Gophers, made the spectacular *Bowery Bugs* (1949, in which Bugs causes Steve Brodie to take his famous leap off the Brooklyn Bridge), and answered that eternal question *What Makes Daffy Duck* (1948). He remained with Friz Freleng's unit as an extraordinary animator after his unit was eliminated, but returned to the director's chair years later to make the delightful *Quackodile Tears* (1962), easily demonstrating that his talent had not dimmed with time.

Norm McCabe also took a turn in the director's chair before returning to animation. He directed such memorable shorts as 1942's *Daffy's Southern Exposure* and *The Ducktators*, a barnyard allegory parodying Hitler's rise to power. McCabe continues to animate for Warner Bros. into the 1990s and has thus been a significant long-term contributor to the Warner Bros. cartoon saga.

Frank Tashlin was one of the greatest and most influential comedy directors of all time—in live action as well as comedy. He later gained fame for his Dean Martin and Jerry Lewis comedies and his 1950s pop-culture parodies, but his touch was equally sure during his various stints at Warner. A significant contributor to the development of Porky Pig in the 1930s, his 1943 *Porky Pig's Feat*, which starred Porky and Daffy (with a cameo appearance by Bugs) remains one of the looniest of the black-and-white Looney Tunes.

Ken Harris, Rudy Larriva, Abe Levitow, Alex Lovy, and Hawley Pratt have also lent their directorial skills to the studio's prodigious

(*Above*) An informal shot of part of Friz Freleng's animation unit, 1954. Standing: Ray Young, Ted Bonnicksen, Gerry Chiniquy. Seated: Art Davis (holding pencil), Sid Farren (right of Davis). Kneeling in front: Bob Matz, Warren Batchelder, John Brandt.

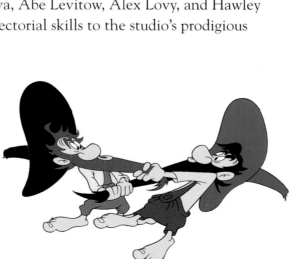

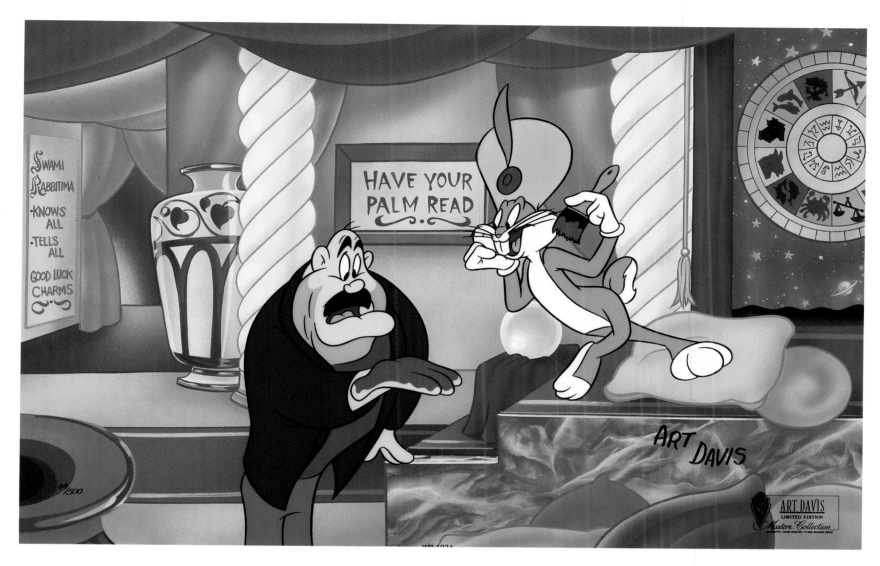

output. One thing is certain about the Warner Bros. cartoon studio: it's never lacked direction.

From decade to decade, the types of animation direction have expanded and broadened. Television specials, directed by David Detiege, Jim Davis, Gerry Chiniquy, Phil Monroe, Greg Ford, Terry Lennon, and Art Vitello have found big audiences in American homes. And theatrical shorts, compilations, commercials, public service announcements, and specialty animation carry the names of directors Greg Ford and Terry Lennon, Darrell Van Citters, Keith Baxter, Douglas McCarthy, Spike Brandt, Tony Cervone, Jeff Siergey, and Frank Molieri.

BOWERY BUGS. Limited Edition. Warner Bros./Art Davis, 1996. Swami Rabbitima sees a bridge in the future for Steve Brody in *Bowery Bugs* (1949), Arthur Davis's only Bugs Bunny cartoon during his short stint as director in the late 1940s.

Additional Artists

Though not a director, Virgil Ross was one of Warner Bros.' "backbone" animators. From his first screen credit for the 1935 Porky Pig cartoon, *Plane Dippy*, through his last 1967 Daffy Duck and Speedy short, *The Spy Swatter* (not to mention his subsequent involvement with Bugs Bunny TV specials and compilation features), Ross helped perpetuate the Warner Bros. animation art style established by Freleng, Avery, Clampett, Jones, and McKimson.

Born in Watertown, New York, Ross was an avid cartoonist during his formative years. He was hired by the Charles Mintz studio in 1930, after it had moved to Hollywood to begin production of sound Krazy Kat cartoons. Within a few short years, Ross went from in-betweening at the Ub Iwerks studio to becoming a full-fledged animator at Walter Lantz, under the tutelage of Tex Avery.

Ross came with Avery to Leon Schlesinger's studio in 1935 and helped establish what would become Warner Bros.' nutty brand of humor. As a key animator in Avery's unit, Ross received screen credit on such classic cartoons as *I Love To Singa* (1936), *Daffy Duck And Egghead* (1938), and *A Wild Hare* (1940), the first Bugs Bunny cartoon. He made his mark as one of the finest and most sensitive character animators at the studio. When Avery left Warners in 1941, Ross joined Bob Clampett's unit and loaned his talents to the delightful Bugs Bunny bond-selling trailer *Any Bonds Today?*. Next, Ross became one of Friz Freleng's key animators from 1944 until the studio temporarily closed in 1963, and was able to put his expertise to use in some of Freleng's best Bugs Bunny, Daffy Duck, and Tweety cartoons. In the Freleng unit, where animator Art Davis was called upon for broad comic action, and the brilliant Gerry Chiniquy demonstrated his knack for meticulously choreographed dance numbers, Ross's unique talents were consistently tapped for scenes of even greater subtlety and psychological complexity—he showed us how the characters *felt*. Sequences such as the jaw-dropping concert animation in the 1946 *Rhapsody Rabbit* (where Ross, an accomplished pianist, shows not just the action of Bugs Bunny playing a piano but seems to convey Bugs's "inner feeling" as he's playing it), Bugs Bunny's spirited telling of his life story in the classic biopic *A Hare Grows in Manhattan* (1947), the rabbit's legendary "Gary Cooper routine" in *Hare Trigger* (1945), Yosemite Sam's smarmy speechifying in *Ballot Box Bunny* (1951), Daffy Duck's act-crabbing envy in *Show Biz Bugs* (1957), and fast action such as Speedy Gonzales' lickety-split charges toward Sylvester are but a few of the standout moments from his quietly dazzling career, where deeply expressive movements always seemed to flow from his pencil point.

Animation writer Warren Foster revises a storyboard sketch. Photograph property of Warner Bros.

Animation writer Tedd Pierce is caught in a staged creative moment. Photograph property of Warner Bros.

Ever an artist, Virgil Ross, a Warner Bros. animator from the early 1930s through the studio's "Golden Age," created his own signed limited-edition cels in the five years before his passing. Photograph property of The Virgil Ross Trust.

LOONEY BIN. Limited Edition. Virgil Ross, 1995.

In the last years before his passing in 1996, Ross created a series of limited-edition signature cels. He also donated his extensive personal animation sketch portfolio to the Warner Bros. Historical Foundation. The collection is housed in the studio archives, and pieces are displayed in the Warner Bros. Museum, as well as other venues around the world.

Part of what makes watching 1950s- and 1960s-era Warner Bros. shorts fun are the fantastic settings. In this phase of the history of Warner Bros. Cartoons, animation design and layout gained increased importance. The stunning graphics supplied by Hawley Pratt (from Friz Freleng's unit) gave a memorably "modernistic" look to cartoons such as *Pizzicato Pussycat* (1955), *Three Little Bops* (1957) and *Birds Anonymous* (1957). Similarly, the work of layout artist Maurice Noble, emerging from Chuck Jones's unit, truly came to the fore during this period. Noble created some of the most unforgettable visual backdrops on film. The elaborate, stylized western deserts in the Road Runner series, his

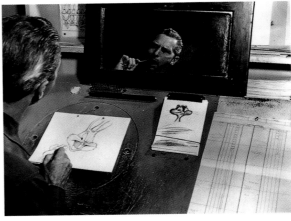

Animator Ken Harris references his own expressions for Bugs Bunny. Photograph property of Warner Bros.

spectacularly wacky futuristic settings in the Marvin The Martian epics, and the pure imagination-gone-wild of the Ralph Phillips daydreams are among his liveliest and most energetic creations. Like Carl Stalling's musical scores, Noble's layouts are abstract fun—uniquely part of a "Warner Bros. Cartoon," and thoroughly entertaining in their own right. No one knows better than Maurice Noble that setting *is* character.

Recruited by the Disney studio during the production of *Snow White and the Seven Dwarfs* in the mid-1930s, Noble became well versed in the ways of animation production during his time as one of Uncle Walt's inspired artists. His first work with Chuck Jones came when Noble joined the Army Signal Corps during World War II, and the two worked together on the *Private Snafu* cartoons for American G.I.s.

In the early 1950s, Noble joined Warner Bros. Cartoons. His presence was felt right from the start, his first Warner screen credit appearing on the classic film *Rabbit Seasoning* (1952). Here, the basic Bunny vs. Duck action took place in a swirl of autumnal colors that seemed to give the dueling duo an extra visual jolt, a real departure from the previous, more naturalistic look of the similarly plotted *Rabbit Fire* (1951). From there, Noble's signature style became unmistakable and can be most clearly seen in such 1950's classics as *Duck Amuck* (1953), *Claws For Alarm* (1954), *Duck Dodgers in the 24 1/2th Century* (1953), and *What's Opera, Doc?* (1957). His work gave Jones's films a striking and identifiable look, far from the realism of Disney, yet certainly distinct from the popular UPA style.

In the 1960s, he went even further. Noble earned co-director status (with Jones) for such one-shot cartoons as *Now Hear This* (1963), with Abe Levitow for *Nelly's Folly* (1961) (both films nominated for Oscars), *Martian Through Georgia* (1962), *I Was A Teenage Thumb* (1963), and the Oscar-winning *The Dot And The Line* (for MGM, 1965), a body of work more akin to the emerging bold designs of independent animation than traditional Hollywood cartoons.

Many of the more current WB Classic Animation artists have utilized their animation skills to create memorable and popular limited-edition cels. Their art has expanded into the limited-edition serigraph/lithograph market, a great example of which is Alan Bodner and Harry Sabin's glamorous black-and-white Looney Tunes "Portrait Series" created under the directive of WB Classic Animation head Kathleen Helppie.

NO MORE PIDDIES. Signed Limited Edition. Virgil Ross, 1992. The helplessness and terror in Sylvester's face tells us everything about the situation—and about Virgil Ross's remarkable ability as an animator.

Music and Sound

arl Stalling underscored the antics of ducks and "wabbits" with a vivid and thoroughly realized musical parallel to the on-screen action. He mixed musical material, seamlessly stitching it together with his own work, making an audio quilt that is greater than the sum of its elaborate patchwork.

Like vocal virtuoso Mel Blanc and the brilliant and resourceful sound effects editor Treg Brown, the other geniuses of the Warner cartoons soundtracks, Stalling started at the studio in 1936, although unlike Blanc he had already spent almost a decade in the animated film business. He had been a silent film accompanist in Kansas City, where he fell in with the young Walt Disney, for whom he toiled at the dawn of movie sound. He had also worked for Ub Iwerks's studio before finally settling in at Warners, where he crafted dozens and dozens of brilliant scores each year, more than six hundred in his career and no two alike.

In scoring the Warner opuses, Stalling pinched and created original melodic material from all manner of sources. He combined excerpts from folk and classical pieces and songs from Warners' own music catalogue (including the already eccentric melodies of Raymond Scott) into a grand melange—brilliantly altering them to suit his purposes. Melody and character and plot all echo each other in a Stalling score: Tweety and the Puddy Tat have a completely different sonic nature than Bugs being chased by Yosemite Sam in the Wild West, or Pepé Le Pew ardently pursuing his elusive love.

After two decades of startling achievement, Stalling gradually retired in the late 1950s, but he has not been forgotten. In the 1990s, Stalling's music was rediscovered when Warner Bros. released two CDs entitled *The Carl Stalling Project I and II*, produced by Greg Ford and Hal Willner. After the release of these CDs, it has been widely acknowledged that Stalling's work is genuine art, worthy of comparison to any twentieth-century composer.

In addition to Stalling, such talents as Frank Marsales, Bernard Brown, Norman Spencer, and Eugene Poddany provided musical scores for Warner Bros. cartoons during its earliest years. But only Milt Franklyn's scores were true heirs to Stalling's masterworks. It's no accident that Franklyn's work stood solidly beside the Stalling classics that preceded it. Franklyn was Stalling's assistant for years before being slowly phased in, from 1953 to 1958, to finally become the studio's official musical director. During the Franklyn era, in a seamless transition, the Coyote's devious plotting, the rascally Rabbit's vengeance, the little black Duck's fevered jealousy, and a certain French skunk's frustrated odor were all accompanied by the familiar orchestral flourishes that were such a major part of Warner cartoons' success.

Composer Carl Stalling created more than six hundred cartoon scores in his career with Warner Bros. Photograph property of Warner Bros.

It was not until the 1960s (a decade of change both inside the studio and out) that a permanent shift in the timbre of the studio's output took place under the direction of William Lava. Caught between the innovative genius of Stalling and the new direction of Lava, Franklyn distinguished himself by providing an extremely high level of craftsmanship that served his collaborators' needs and the cartoon audience as well.

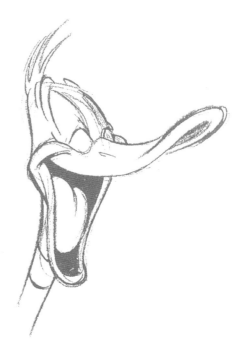

Though animated cartoons are quintessentially a visual medium, Warner Bros.' dominance of the animated short came not just through sight but also through sound. Mel Blanc was the greatest voice artist of his or any time. Carl Stalling was unsurpassed at creating a cartoon's musical score. And sound wizard Tregoweth "Treg" Brown gave Warner cartoons a sonic dimension unparalleled in the field. There is an inside joke in the Chuck Jones classic *One Froggy Evening* in which a building's cornerstone identifies the structure as the "Tregoweth Brown Building." The allusion has real significance, since Brown was truly a cornerstone of the Warner cartoon studio.

Erroneously credited as "film editor," Treg Brown was the man behind the Looney Tunes and Merrie Melodies sound from 1934 until the studio temporarily shut the animation department's doors in the early 1960s. Whenever there was a "beowoop!" or a "boink!", the "thunk-thunk-thunk" of the Road Runner's tongue or the vibrato of a buzzard's larynx on the soundtrack of a Warner Bros. cartoon, it was Brown who put it there. His comedically transcendent efforts combined Mel Blanc's vocal characterizations, Carl Stalling's whimsical symphonies, and his own clanks, flutters, whirrs, and mortar shots into finished soundtracks that forever defined cartoon sound. (It was Brown who actually hired Mel Blanc, so his influence on the auditory end of the studio's output goes far beyond his brilliant creation and employment of effects.) And when artisans of the modern era try to recreate the aural effects of animation's Golden Age, it is always the Treg Brown sound they are striving for.

A person's voice tells much about his or her personality—through inflection, diction, and quirks of speech. Amazingly, Mel Blanc was able to create not just voices but also personalities through the controlled vibration of a pair of world-class vocal cords. Blanc's vocal creations are a virtual audio catalog of entities. It's hardly surprising that he was able to rise to the top of the two media that required non-visual acting—cartoons and radio. Simply put, Mel Blanc was the greatest "voice artist" in the history of show business.

When he went to work for Warner Bros. in the mid-1930s, Blanc's first major chore was to come up with a workable voice for Porky Pig. Previously, the pig's stammer had been uncontollable since it was a real stutterer doing the voice. But Blanc could serve it up at will, making the stutter—and the character—lovable and comical. His work was recognized by his studio colleagues as indispensable, and in 1940 Leon Schlesinger signed the actor to a contract that made Blanc exclusive to Warners in the cartoon field. (In 1939, Blanc also became a regular multicharacter player on "The Jack Benny Show," the best-remembered series in the history of radio.)

There are too many masterpieces of "voice characterization" in Blanc's lengthy career to cite more than a few. His contrasting of Bugs against the perennially self-congratulating super genius, Wile E. Coyote, in *Operation: Rabbit* surely stands out, as do the Blanc/Bugs excursions into the world of longhair music in *Rabbit of Seville* and *What's Opera, Doc?*

Blanc remained with Warners' cartoon unit until his death in 1989. In later years, he enlivened countless commercials, specials, and compilation features with his unique and magical touch. He also became a goodwill ambassador for Warner Bros., making many personal appearances and embodying the spirit of days gone by. The man himself may now be gone, but his talent is eternally preserved in a menagerie of sidesplitting characters. In the words of Jack Benny, Mel was "the man of a thousand voices."

Mel Blanc may have been the man of a thousand voices, but at Warner Bros. he was aided and abetted by a talented ensemble no less individually auspicious. The foremost of these was Arthur Q. Bryan, who—though he could plausibly be termed the man of one voice—supplied vocal characterizations second only to Blanc's in importance to the cartoons. That's because Bryan performed the voice of Elmer Fudd, a role so indispensable that after his death in 1959—though Dave Barry, Hal Smith, and even Blanc himself later attempted the role—few could capture it quite like Bryan.

Also of paramount importance were Sara Berner, Bea Benaderet, and June Foray, who portrayed the majority of the studio's female characters (including the ever-elderly Granny). The great comedian, puppeteer, and adman Stan Freberg comes next, having supplied many of the studio's non-Blanc male voices since he was a teen. He was one of the Goofy Gophers, played the sycophantic "Chester" to Blanc's burly "Spike" in Freleng's *Tree For Two*, assayed the moronic and oversized "Junyer Bear" character in Jones's Three Bears series, giggled his way through half a dozen Hubie and Bertie cartoons (he's Bertie, sure-sure), and even supplied his dulcet tones to the amusingly dimwitted Pete Puma.

Story man Tedd Pierce and director Tex Avery also provided many Warner Bros. vocal delights, especially Pierce's exhilaratingly apt emulation of straight man supreme Bud Abbott and Avery's trademark demonic laugh. Daws Butler was likewise a favorite—most particularly in *The Honey-Mousers*. Narrator Robert C. Bruce, radio comedians Danny Webb, Kent Rogers, Jim Backus, and comic Larry Storch are only a few of the many actors who gave numerous vocal performances in support—even big-time celebrities Jack Benny and Victor Moore played a part in the studio's vocal shenanigans over the years and should receive their due for the pleasure they've brought audiences across the decades.

Mel Blanc performs to the amusement and direction of Robert McKimson, c. 1959. Photograph property of Warner Bros.

BUGS BUNNY

DAFFY DUCK

ELMER FUDD

PORKY PIG

SYLVESTER & TWEETY

YOSEMITE SAM

MICHIGAN J. FROG

THE TASMANIAN DEVIL

SPEEDY GONZALES

PEPÉ LE PEW

THE ROAD RUNNER
 & WILE E. COYOTE

FOGHORN LEGHORN

MARVIN THE MARTIAN

THE PLAYERS

Bugs Bunny

Bugs Bunny was cool long before Brando was cool, a rebel a generation earlier than James Dean, and his snappy, nasal New York accent was a cultural beacon in an era when the movies were beamed strictly to middle-American tastes.

The rabbit's monicker may have sprung from the nickname from Ben "Bugs" Hardaway, which happened to be 1930s slang for "slightly nuts."

Bugs debuted in Tex Avery's 1940 classic *A Wild Hare*. Here was an animated personality the likes of which had never been seen before: calculating, yet with a lingering touch of the screwball, born to tease and "heckle" the Fudd-figure, who has the misfortune of trying to hunt him, yet capable of feeling sorry for the poor dope at the same time. Bugs not only fares well against "maroons" like Red Hot Ryder in Bob Clampett's *Buckaroo Bugs* but is also more than up to reducing a "super genius" such as Wile E. Coyote into a blithering idiot in Chuck Jones's *Operation: Rabbit*. Bugs vanquished many adversaries, but the rabbit's integrity and self-possession were such that he didn't necessarily *need* a foil to strut his

(Previous spread) LOONEY TUNES ON PARADE. Limited Edition. Warner Bros. Classic Animation (characters) and Warner Bros. Animation Art Program (backgrounds), 1993. The most famous lineup in cartoon history.

BUGS MODEL SHEET. Limited Edition. Bob Clampett, 1991.

WHAT'S COOKIN', DOC? Limited Edition. Bob Clampett, 1990. Upon receiving a rabbit-shaped "booby prize" from the Motion Picture Academy, a grateful Bugs vows to keep it and cherish it, even take it to bed with him every night—little dreaming that the coy statuette would take that promise in quite a different fashion! From *What's Cookin' Doc?* (1944).

stuff, as amply demonstrated by a number of key Freleng pics: whether pounding the keyboard as a tuxedoed concert pianist (*Rhapsody Rabbit*), executing a wicked samba under a nightclub spotlight (*Slick Hare*), or singing and dancing his way down the streets of old New York (*A Hare Grows in Manhattan*), Bugs was a solo performer of rare grace and panache. Above all, Bugs was completely three-dimensional in his emotional makeup and, throughout more than 175 classic cartoons, always believable.

Embraced as the symbol of plucky Americanism in the war years, Bugs became the epitome of cool by the 1950s, a period in which he was cast against such excitable foils as Yosemite Sam (in his only Oscar-winner, Freleng's *Knighty Knight Bugs*), Jones's Marvin The Martian, McKimson's Tasmanian Devil, and Daffy Duck, as well as old reliable Elmer Fudd (co-star of Chuck Jones's ambitious Wagner spoof, *What's Opera, Doc?*). Like Jack Benny, here's a showman who barely has to look at his audience to move them to wild applause (as in Freleng's *Show Biz Bugs*). If the essence of decades and decades of everything that was great about the Warner cartoons could be distilled into a single character, it would be Bugs Bunny.

(*Above*) WHAT'S COOKIN' DOC? Signed Limited Edition. Friz Freleng, 1992. Friz Freleng's Bugs was a connoisseur not only of music but of carrots, too.

(*Below*) THE OLD GREY HARE. Limited Edition. Warner Bros. Classic Animation, 1990. Created by Warner Bros. Classic Animation for Bugs Bunny's 50th Anniversary (Special Edition). Little Old Man Bugs throttles Little Old Man Elmer in a scene from *The Old Grey Hare*, which effectively illustrates the tendencies of Bob Clampett and animator Rod Scribner to take their characters to hilariously ludicrous extremes.

(*Above*) LITTLE RED RIDING RABBIT. Signed Limited
Edition. Virgil Ross, 1994. Director Friz Freleng's 1944 re-
telling of the Red Riding Hood story (with Red now an
irksome bobby-soxer that Bugs can't stand, and Granny
working swingshift at Lockheed) is this image's inspiration.

(*Right*) BUGS BUNNY GETS THE BOID. Limited Edition. Bob
Clampett, 1989. In 1942, "getting the bird" was the same thing
as getting a "Bronx cheer." Obviously, the only ones cheering
in 1942 were audiences as Bugs plays with the synapse-
challenged Beaky Buzzard and his musical Adam's apple.

(*Above*) BUGS AND CRUSHER. Signed Limited Edition. Chuck Jones, 1995. Brains beat brawn any day, as Chuck Jones made eminently clear in his 1951 short *Bunny Hugged*, from which this limited-edition cel was inspired.

(*Opposite, top*) MISSISSIPPI HARE. Signed Limited Edition. Chuck Jones, 1991. Bugs is an instant master of any undertaking he attempts (and that extends to gambling) when his cotton tail lands him on an Old South riverboat in Chuck Jones's masterful, *Mississippi Hare* (1949).

(*Opposite, bottom*) HAIR-RAISING HARE. Signed Limited Edition. Chuck Jones, 1995. Bugs and "Gossamer" are joined by a Peter Lorre-like mad scientist and a mechanical sweetheart in this tableau based on the 1946 Chuck Jones short.

© Warner Bros Inc. 1991
46/100   Chuck Jones

More brief encounters with friends and foes:
(*Left, top*) ABOMINABLE SNOW BUNNY. Signed Limited Edition. Chuck Jones, 1996. In Jones's 1961 short (co-directed by Maurice Noble), Bugs and Daffy battle it out using the moronic Abominable Snow Man as a foil. In this image derived from the cartoon, apparently Daffy is ahead.

(*Left, middle*) A-LAD-IN HIS LAMP. Limited Edition. Warner Bros. Classic Animation, 1990. Created by Warner Bros. Classic Animation for Bugs Bunny's 50th Anniversary (Special Collection), this scene depicts the Jim Backus–voiced genie and his "little bucktoothed pal" in McKimson's *A-Lad-In His Lamp*.

(*Left, bottom*) CHEZ BUGS. Limited Edition. Warner Bros., 1996. Those wacky Gaulish chefs, Francois and Louie—pink tomato noses and all—learn cooking from the inside out in McKimson's *French Rarebit*.

Daffy Duck

"oo-woo-hoo! Hoo-hoo! Hoo-hoo! Hoo-hoo!"

He was the first cartoon character to be christened after an eccentric state of mental hyperactivity (making him a nominal forerunner to "Bugs" Bunny and "Screwy" Squirrel). Thus it might be considered "typical of the little black Duck" that he could be diagnosed with a very specific neurosis—a split personality. That's because there were at least two Daffy Duck characters in different periods of his career, the first maniacally manic and the second despicably depressive.

The original Daffy, introduced in 1937 in *Porky's Duck Hunt*, was also the first animated entity to exalt in wackiness strictly for its own sake. Where radio comic Joe Penner represented live-action Hollywood's idea of a screwball, Tex Avery, by comparison, casts his screwball "Egghead" as straight man to Daffy's batty antics (in *Daffy Duck and Egghead*). Forever emitting manic cries of "hoo-hoo!", the Duck is empowered by his insanity: explaining his ability to ride through the air

(*Above*) THE RACE IS ON! Signed Limited Edition. Chuck Jones, 1983. Daffy Duck in a characteristically high-energy pose, always moving, always *explaining*.

(*Left*) DAFFY PERSONA. Limited Edition. Warner Bros., 1995. The many phases of Daffy Duck: Poses from *Duck Dodgers in the 24 1/2th Century*, *The Great Piggy Bank Robbery*, *Book Revue*, *Duck Amuck*, *Drip-Along Daffy*, and *Yankee Doodle Daffy*

on an imaginary tricycle in *Porky & Daffy*, he babbles, "I'm so crazy, I don't know this is impossible."

In many ways, Daffy reached his peak in the mid-1940s, when he was still crazy, but slowly beginning to discover a devious streak. He interrupts his craziness to cringe at the prospect of induction in Bob Clampett's *Draftee Daffy*, but is more than willing to put his wackiness at the service of Uncle Sam in Friz Freleng's *Daffy—The Commando*. In the Freleng masterpiece *Yankee Doodle Daffy*, he's everything at once: crazy, conniving, and a song-and-dance man to rival George M. Cohan.

Still, the Daffy everyone remembers best is the deceitful Duck, refined and perfected by Chuck Jones in the early 1950s, the hapless schemer whose efforts to outdo his rivals (particularly Bugs Bunny) inevitably blow up in his face. 1953's *Duck Amuck* is not only Jones's most hysterical deconstruction of cinematic conventions, but a *tour de force* of paranoid performance art for its star. From this point on, Daffy becomes an easily exasperated heavy—mainly in the 1960s, against Speedy Gonzales. Daffy is perenially uncool, feeling frustrated and "out of the loop" in every era. He is as jealous of co-star Porky Pig in Freleng's 1940 classic *You Ought To Be In Pictures* as he is envious of Bugs Bunny sixteen years later in the same director's behind-the-scenes *A Star Is Bored*. While Bugs instinctively knows how to marshal all the principles of space and time to his benefit, Daffy sees himself lined up against a merciless universe, fighting back with whatever inadequate defense he can muster, from out-and-out madness to cranky defiance.

No matter how much his cohorts upstage him, most painfully in Freleng's *Show Biz Bugs*, Daffy is undeniably a star, second only to Bugs himself. Not bad for a neurotic waterfowl who began life (as identified on his first model sheet) as a mere "crazy, darn fool duck."

(*Above*) PAR FOR THE COURSE. Signed Limited Edition. Friz Freleng, 1994. Who knows—this may be a "cymbal-ic" scene from an unproduced Bugs and Daffy golf epic entitled *Putt, Rabbit, Putt.*

(*Below*) DAFFY FINDS HIS PIGGYBANK. Limited Edition. Bob Clampett, 1990. "Duck Twacy" at last finds the object of his fetishistic adoration, his own little piggybank, held captive in a vault by a roomful of screwy, Gould-ish comic strip villains.

THE GREAT PIGGY BANK ROBBERY. Limited Edition. Bob
Clampett, 1989. "Duck Twacy" encounters a de-tek-it-tive
even more famous than himself in this literary encounter in
Bob Clampett's major mallard masterpiece, *The Great Piggy
Bank Robbery*.

(Above) DAFFY SHERLOCK AND YOSEMITE. Signed Limited Edition. Chuck Jones, 1989. Never have clues been sought by two so utterly clueless in this lighthearted pose from Chuck Jones.

(Left) BUGS THE STAR. Signed Limited Edition. Friz Freleng, 1990. Inspired by Freleng's own *A Star Is Bored* (1956), this image shows what happens when Daffy wishes that his career would pick up.

(Opposite) LUNACY. Signed Limited Edition. Chuck Jones, 1982. Chuck Jones's official portrait of the Duck as Duck Dodgers—he of the 24 1/2th century, futuristic hero of many an exciting space adventure—and his "eager young space cadet" assistant, played by old pal Porky Pig.

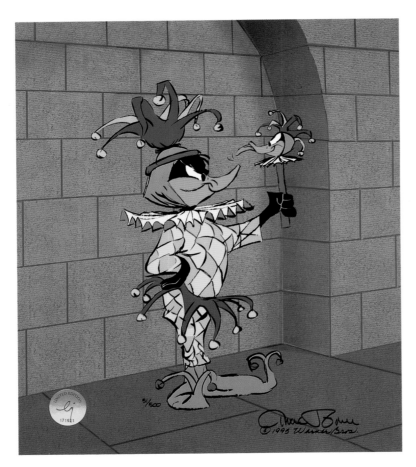

(*Above*) RABBIT FIRE. Limited Edition. Warner Bros. Classic Animation, 1990. Created by Warner Bros. Classic Animation for Bugs Bunny's 50th Anniversary (Special Collection), Chuck Jones's most "wubbulous" of wacky waterfowl is a bird with a blown-about beak in *Rabbit Fire*.

(*Left*) RUDE JESTER. Signed Limited Edition. Chuck Jones, 1995. Daffy, particularly perturbed in ruffles and bells, is not the most jolly of court jesters.

DAFFY BEAKHEAD. Signed Limited Edition. Chuck Jones, 1993. Daffy discovers yet more humiliating ways in which his anatomy can be distorted by the firing of Elmer's rifle in Chuck Jones's inspired trilogy of Duck-Rabbit-Hunter encounters, *Rabbit Fire*, *Rabbit Seasoning*, and *Duck! Rabbit, Duck!*

SOUND PLEASE. Signed Limited Edition. Chuck Jones, 1993.
An irate Daffy giving instructions to the animator
controlling his destiny in *Duck Amuck*.

NASTY CANASTA. Signed Limited Edition. Chuck Jones, 1995. Even as western lawman *Drip-Along Daffy*, our hero is always getting on the short end of the situation, like in this encounter with rustler, bandit, and square-dance caller Nasty Canasta.

Elmer Fudd

The most lasting image of Elmer Fudd is of a poor sap, so pathetic that he fairly begs to be heckled. Or worse. Indeed, for years the Looney Tunes-smiths made Elmer so ridiculous—what with his baby-like enunciation ("wabbit" has pwactically wepwaced "rabbit" in the dictionary), simpering chuckle, (heh-heh-heh!), and his beautiful head of skin—that no one in the audience, let alone a fellow cartoon character, could resist the urge to tease him mercilessly. Nothing is lower than Elmer on the animation universe's evolutionary scale. He's rendered helpless by an army of ants in Freleng's *Ant Pasted*, and even inanimate objects (such as a persistent candle in Jones's *Good Night Elmer*) have the ability to reduce Fudd to a state of blithering idiocy.

At the end of the 1930s, the hunting scenario had evolved into the studio's favorite format, launching both of its biggest stars, Daffy Duck and Bugs Bunny. It became clear that if the Duck and the Rabbit were to have any endurance, they needed an appropriate foil, a "heavy" who was, in a sense, aggressively passive. The point of the hunting format, of course, was that the tables are turned—the intended prey turns out to be screwy and makes life miserable for the hunter. Elmer Fudd began life in 1940 in *Elmer's Candid Camera*, and by Avery's *A Wild Hare*, was perfected as the studio's ultimate patsy.

The amazing thing about the Elmer-hunting-Bugs formula was that the instant that the studio perfected it, they started turning it on its ear (hilariously in Clampett's *The Old Grey Hare*, where both characters flash-forward fifty years into the future and go through all their usual sassy routines as lumbago-ridden octogenarians). By the 1950s, the hunting theme had led to dozens of variations, most memorably Chuck Jones's threesome of threesomes (beginning with *Rabbit Fire*) wherein Bugs and Daffy each try to goad Elmer into blasting the other, in Freleng's hysterical *Stage Door Cartoon*, which brought the hunt straight from the forest into a burlesque house and humiliatingly cast a red-faced Fudd as an unwilling striptease artist, and McKimson's masterpiece, *What's Up Doc?*, which further illustrated that the whole hunting-and-heckling bit may have had its origins in vaudeville. Jones's *What's Opera, Doc?* finds the format grandly transplanted into Wagnerian Valhalla, while Freleng's *Hare Brush* definitively re-reverses the standard Fudd format: only by becoming a "scwewy wabbit" himself does Elmer Fudd finally get the best of Bugs.

(*Top*) I Give Up Season. Signed Limited Edition. Chuck Jones, 1993.

(*Above*) Identity Cwisis. Sericel. Warner Bros., 1991. Two moments arising from the Bugs-Daffy-Elmer hunting cycle: three great characters united in great cartoons that are, above all, triumphs of Euclidian logic. As soon as one character establishes a designated hunting season for a specific animal, then that character, invariably Daffy, is blasted by Fudd's shooting iron.

GROUCHO BUGS. Limited Edition. Robert McKimson, 1993. Bugs and Elmer were a partnership not only for all seasons but for all media. By 1956's *Wideo Wabbit* (directed by Bob McKimson) they were taking their teaming to a new level when Fudd becomes host of a hunting program in pursuit of the wabbit, who mimics a slew of celebrities, including TV's most famous Marx brother.

(*Above*) FIGARO FERTILIZER. Sericel. Chuck Jones, 1992. It's
the look of anticipation on Elmer's face—the thought for just
an instant that he might actually be growing hair on his most
capitol dome—just before the curly locks blossom into
flowers, that makes the whole *Seville* gag work.

(*Opposite, top*) DANCES WITH WABBITS. Signed Limited
Edition. Chuck Jones, 1991. It's anyone's guess how long
before the dance turns into a chase.

(*Opposite, bottom*) RABBIT OF SEVILLE (V). Signed Limited
Edition. Chuck Jones, 1995. This scene inspired by Jones's
cartoon shows how Bugs can charm anything—even an
electric shaver—into tormenting the hapless Elmer Fudd.

AP/500
©Warner Bros. Inc. 1988

WHAT'S OPERA, DOC? (III). Signed Limited Edition.
Chuck Jones, 1989. Both Elmer's and Bugs's careers climax
with Jones's most classical of masterpieces, the Wagner-
inspired *What's Opera, Doc?* This 1957 epic satirizes the
grand tradition of Viking opera and also manages to rib an
entire century of ballet in the process.

Porky Pig

He is the pig of our hearts, and the studio's first enduring star. During his heyday as the Looney Tunes' leading player from 1936 to 1940, Porky had a childlike demeanor (never more so than in the sentimentally patriotic *Old Glory*, 1939) or, at least, an innocent. When Porky's own series later gave birth to those of his successors Daffy Duck and Bugs Bunny, the Pig spent much of the 1940s in the unlikely role of hunter or beleaguered homeowner By the 1950s, however, Porky came into his own again, this time as a straight man.

Porky is forever at the service of the screwballs placed around him (not only Daffy Duck but the insane inhabitants of *Porky in Wackyland*, 1938) as well as his directors' aspirations: Tashlin's cinematic ambitions (*Case Of The Stuttering Pig*, 1937), Avery's logical lunacy (*The Blow Out*, 1936), and Clampett's juxtaposition of coyness and wackiness (*Porky's Tire Trouble*, 1939). Porky was even rudely thrust into the world of "real life" in Freleng's *You Ought To Be In Pictures* (1940), which showed the pig speeding in a car down a live-action steet in the middle of "rush-hour" traffic, stampeded by a live-action herd of galloping horses, and (maybe scariest of all) locked in a contract dispute with his real-life boss Leon Schlesinger. And throughout it all, he stuttered: never was a speech

PORKY MODEL SHEET. Limited Edition. Bob Clampett, 1991. The Perfect Porky, or, A Pig For All Reasons: This collection of 1940s poses captures the grandeur of both of Porky's most celebrated directors, Clampett and Jones.

impediment rendered so lovingly than by the studio's resident voice genius, Mel Blanc. In fact, Porky's attempts to pronounce "That's all, folks!" became the studio's number one audio trademark.

But neither Blanc nor Porky's patented cuteness were present in the character's debut outing, the 1935 color Merrie Melodies, *I Haven't Got A Hat*, directed by Friz Freleng. Porky was eventually moved from the early color Merrie Melodies series over to the black-and-white Looney Tunes series, and, by 1936, with Blanc (not to mention Avery, Tashlin, and Clampett) in place, and solidly launched by *I Haven't Got A Hat*, the first great phase of Looney Tunes began.

Born again at the end of the 1940s, Porky was reconceived by Chuck Jones as a "fussy bachelor type" (writer Mike Maltese's description) who functions as a key contrast for the over-emotionally needy Charlie Dog (*Often An Orphan*, 1949) and a doubting Thomas who refuses to believe his own cat, Sylvester, in his claims of killer mice and Martians (*Scaredy Cat*, 1948; *Jumpin' Jupiter*, 1955). But the Pig really shines in cool counterpoint to Daffy's histrionics in Jones's glorious genre parodies, particularly *Drip-Along Daffy* (1951), *Deduce, You Say* (1956), and *Duck Dodgers in the 24 1/2th Century* (1953). After years of standing by idly as relative second-bananas grabbed the spotlight, at last Porky Pig was elevated to the status of the sidekick who steals the show.

INFORMATION ABOUT THE DO-DO. Limited Edition. Bob Clampett, 1991. Porky finds only more confusion when he asks a simple question of the Do-do in *Porky in Wackyland*.

Woo-Woo! Limited Edition. Bob Clampett, 1991. Lewis
Carroll takes on a decidedly Looney Tunes twist in Bob
Clampett's brilliant *Porky in Wackyland*, in which the Pig
chases the valuable "Do-do" Bird—who's as rare as he is
batty—across a surrealistic, Dali-esque landscape.

GROUNDHOG'S DAY. Limited Edition. Robert McKimson,
1993. In Bob McKimson's chubby-cheeked classic *One Meat
Brawl*, the Pig goes hunting again (this time in response to
the post-war meat shortage) in pursuit of that most endearing
of one-shot antagonists, Grover Groundhog, and supported
by a dog he calls "Mandrake," who would spend the 1950s in
the company of Foghorn Leghorn, bereft of any appellation.

Sylvester & Tweety

Clampett's canary spoke in baby talk, Freleng's cat (like a certain duck before him) inherited a lisp from Warner boss Leon Schlesinger. They became Warners' greatest long-running team. When the right bird and right cat finally locked horns in their big team-up in 1947's Oscar-winning *Tweetie Pie* (in which Sylvester was named "Thomas"), director Friz Freleng knew he had just united the the Warner studio's own dream team.

From that point on, it was Bird vs. Cat in an almost uncountable number of episodes, a struggle that carried them across six decades and the farthest corners of the globe. And it was always Sylvester's own deviousness and bad luck that did him in, while Tweety's childlike

TWEETY MODEL SHEET. Limited Edition. Bob Clampett, 1991. A variety of images of Tweety, "the naked genius himself," as shown in this limited edition cel from Bob Clampett. Note the baby-like features, the big eyes, pouty lips, and bald cranium—*looks* perfectly innocent!

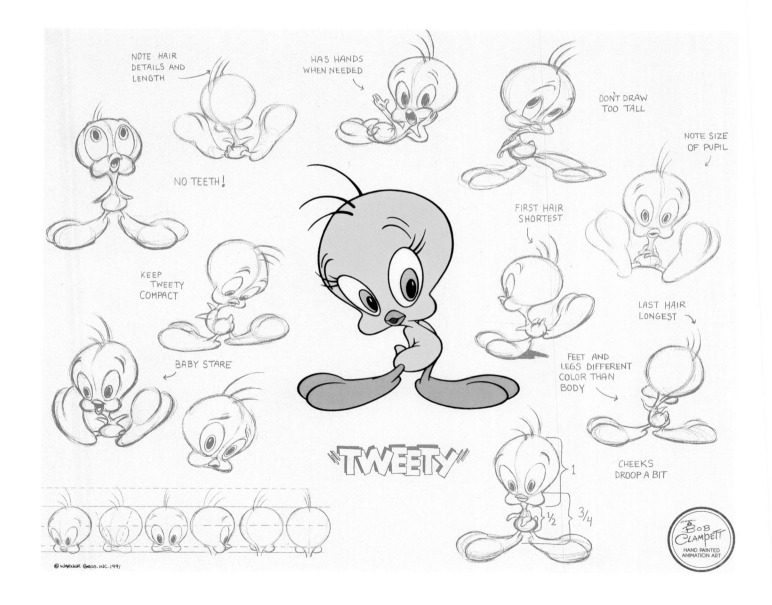

innocence (and brutal sense of self-preservation) kept him out of the cat's stomach.

And just as in the 1930s there was often Ginger without Fred but rarely Fred without Ginger, Sylvester made many appearances on his own. Indeed, he enjoyed two birdless sub-careers chasing mice: the giant rodent (actually baby kangaroo) Hippety Hopper (in a series created by Robert McKimson that co-starred the Cat's easily embarrassed son, Sylvester, Jr.) and the super-fast Mexicali mouse, Speedy Gonzales. Sylvester turned in a virtuoso song-and-dance performance as a one-cat-band in the Freleng musicomedy *Back Alley Oproar* (1948), and even more hilarious was the cat's solo masterpiece of feline frustration, Freleng's 1951 *Canned Feud*. But the *pièces de résistance* of pussycat pictures were always the Bird-and-Cat episodes, none more so than Freleng's (and Warren Foster's) ace noir parody of 12-step-program life, *Birds Anonymous* (1957).

CLASSIC TWEETY. Limited Edition. Bob Clampett, 1986.

GOT HIM. Signed Limited Edition. Friz Freleng, 1993.
Freleng's Tweety and Sylvester gags became part of the
lexicon of screen comedy. A typical scene: Sylvester finally
getting into the birdcage and finding an inhabitant
other than the helpless little yellow baby bird he expected.
Atypically, a tittering Granny is in on the gag.

(*Above*) BIRDY AND THE BEAST. Limited Edition. Bob
Clampett, 1989. If you think it looks bad for Tweety in this
particular image based on Clampett's 1944 short of the same
name, you don't know him vewwy well, do you?

(*Opposite*) BIRDS ANONYMOUS. Signed Limited Edition.
Friz Freleng, 1991. While Hollywood was melodramatizing
the Alcoholics Anonymous group with lachrymose features
like *I'll Cry Tomorrow*, leave it to a comic genius like Friz
Freleng to find the humor in substance addiction. In
Sylvester and Tweety's second Oscar winner, *Birds
Anonymous* (it was Friz's third!), he turns a potentially
morbid situation into a hysterical one, as a "sobriety"-
espousing feline friend tries to prevent Sylvester from "falling
off the wagon" and consuming Tweety.

THE POUNCE. Signed Limited Edition. Virgil Ross, 1992.
Sylvester's best move is broken down into its component
parts by veteran animator Virgil Ross.

SYLVESTER'S BUFFET. Signed Limited Edition. Friz Freleng, 1994. Sylvester in his usual role as garbage-can connoisseur, a pose he assumed many times beginning with his premiere appearance in 1945's *Life With Feathers*, directed by Freleng. This time, however, something new has been added: unbeknownst to our feline hero, the object of his appetite sits perched on his plate, while his worst nightmare awaits him in an adjacent can.

Yosemite Sam

Great horny toads!

"I was looking for a character strong enough to work against Bugs," Friz Freleng recollected. "Elmer [Fudd] wasn't it. So I thought to use the smallest guy I could think of along with the biggest voice I could get." In contrast to the passive Fuddy-duddiness of the hapless Elmer, Yosemite Sam provided a far more energetic (and dangerous) foil for Bugs Bunny. Elmer's humor is slow burn style, while Yosemite Sam's is fast and furious. Where Elmer's patience is continually tested, Yosemite Sam never has any to begin with. Yet Yosemite Sam's furry face is as much an icon of the rabbit pictures as Fudd's hairless dome.

Yosemite Sam is first seen as a train robber who's as plum ornery as he is short in the 1945 *Hare Trigger*, one of the early Bugs Bunny westerns. Diminutive and blustery, the story in animation circles was that Yosemite Sam was the cartoon incarnation of Freleng himself, a rumor which apparently delighted Freleng, who directed all but two of the Bugs/Yosemite Sam cartoons. In the beginning, Yosemite Sam appears primarily in traditional masculine adventure settings—not just in westerns (*Bugs Bunny Rides Again*, 1948), but on pirate ships (*Mutiny on the Bunny*,

SAHARA SAM. Signed Limited Edition. Friz Freleng, 1993. Yosemite Sam's efforts to start and stop his beasts of burden (like those of his predecessor, Red Hot Ryder in *Buckaroo Bugs*) may seem a bit on the extreme side, but the only way this particular camel will stop and start is when Yosemite Sam whacks him soundly with his rifle. Incidentally, the name "Riff Raff Sam," here in *Sahara Hare*, is a play on the tribal name from Warners' early talkie, *The Desert Song*.

THE BIG SNEEZE. Signed Limited Edition. Friz Freleng,
1994. More attempts to control animals: In his role as the
nemesis of director Freleng's *Knighty Knight Bugs*, "The Black
Knight" (Yosemite Sam) must contend with yet another
slow-responding animal—this one's a fire-breathing dragon,
whose case of the hiccups results in random incinerations.

1950), in the American Revolution (*Bunker Hill Bunny*, 1950), and in the Klondike (*14 Carrot Rabbit*, 1952). Eventually Bugs and Yosemite Sam will have it out in all manner of contexts, battling for money (*From Hare to Heir*, 1960), love (*Hare Trimmed*, 1953), political power (*Ballot Box Bunny*, 1951), real estate (*Fair-Haired Hare*, 1951), and genuine war (civil, that is, in *Southern Fried Rabbit*, 1953). Bugs and Yosemite Sam also battled it out in ancient Rome, the French Foreign Legion, and even the Middle Ages (*Knighty Knight Bugs*, 1958, Bugs Bunny's only Oscar-winning short).

"We didn't try to make [Yosemite Sam] likable," Freleng continued. "We did just the opposite. We made him the meanest character in the whole world. But [audiences] liked him in spite of that. Guys like Yosemite Sam snapped up your motion picture, because he was such a violent character, and he didn't have to stop and think and plot." Always a bandit at heart—even when cast as a foreign legionnaire, a knight, or an ancient Roman centurion—Yosemite Sam's first objective was to steal your attention. Volatile, unstable, and absolutely unable to turn away from a challenge, Yosemite Sam's personality was always like nitroglycerine—it didn't take much shaking to make it explode. You'd expect no less from the guy who brought the terms "galoot" and "varmint" into the national lexicon—the roughest-toughest hombre west of the Rio Grande (and he didn't mean Mahatma Gandhi).

(Below, left) RIDE 'EM SAM. Signed Limited Edition. Friz Freleng, 1994. A classic pose of Yosemite Sam atop one of his characteristically uncooperative "varmints."

(Below, right) NO SMOKING. Signed Limited Edition. Friz Freleng, 1991. Nothing sets off a knight's temper more than a sneezing fire-breathing dragon, as shown in this image inspired by Freleng's Oscar-winning *Knighty Knight Bugs*.

(Opposite) TRIBUTE TO FRIZ. Limited Edition. Warner Bros., 1996. This loving limited-edition tribute to Friz Freleng gives his creation, Yosemite Sam, a chance to do something he rarely, if ever, managed on screen: ride off into the sunset in a happy ending. For once he's presumably mounted on a steed that will actually obey his command to "Who-o-a!"

Michigan J. Frog

Michigan J. Frog stands as the sole example of a character who became internationally famous, a corporate symbol no less, after appearing in only a single theatrical cartoon. Then again, the image of the frog in that classic film, *One Froggy Evening* (1955), is impossible to forget. A construction worker, in the middle of demolishing an archaic, decrepit building, pries open its long-sealed cornerstone and out pops—a frog. Now, any hundred-year-old frog still living, presumably without food or water, for lo these many decades would be news. But there's an additional hook: outfitted with top hat and cane, the frog makes like a Gay Nineties vaudevillian, belting a jingle of the early technological era, "Hello My Baby" (". . . send me a kiss by wire"). But this golden opportunity is soon revealed to be a charade. Not realizing the frog will sing only for him, our working-class hero gradually succumbs to insanity and destitution in his luckless attempts to exploit this miracle he's found.

By director Chuck Jones's own definition, *One Froggy Evening* is pure farce, which he describes as "real people in funny situations." (This he distinguishes from "comedy," which is "funny people in real situations," i.e., Elmer hunting Bugs). Jones sets the picture not in the cartooniverse of stuttering pigs and despicable ducks, but in an all-human "real" world where singing frogs do not often appear. To make the frog appear all the more remarkable, Jones and writer Michael Maltese tell this whole story sans dialogue—the only voice on the soundtrack is that of the frog and his antiquated arias (among them Maltese's original, "Michigan Rag," the song that eventually named the character).

Perhaps that's part of the secret of the frog's endless appeal—he's doubly unreal, even in a cartoon context. And that's why this singing frog, set to motion by the WB Classic Animation department, was used to help establish the look of the fledgling Warner Bros. network, The WB. In the media-conscious 90s, Michigan J. Frog is the cartoon character's cartoon character.

RIBET. Sericel. Warner Bros., 1995. Michigan J. Frog no more. As soon as a third party enters the scene, the magical amphibian reverts to a decidely unanthropomorphic pond denizen, looking completely out of place with his miniature hat and cane, and emitting froggy noises instead of turn-of-the-century ragtime numbers in a beautiful baritone.

HAT HAS TWO TONE HI-LITE

ON ALL FOURS IN DORMANT STATE

ELEVATED PINKY DENOTES SOPHISTICATED SHOWMANSHIP

KEEP CENTER LINE ON BELLY TO SHOW FORM

LOWER LIP OVERLAPS

KEEP FINGERS AND TOES THIN

NOTE SLIGHT HUMPBACK

Michigan J. Frog

IN EXTREME POSES MOUTH CAN BE 2/3'S SIZE OF BODY

USE BROWS FOR EXPRESSION

SLIGHT BELLY

644/750

LIMITED EDITION
© 1995 Warner Bros.

MICHIGAN J. FROG MODEL SHEET. Limited Edition, Warner Bros., 1995. Chuck Jones's Michigan J. Frog in action, and as the poses in the upper right-hand corner reveal, in an equally important state of inaction. This model chart clearly illuminates the vast discrepancy between the frog as song-and-dance man and the frog as just plain frog.

MICHIGAN J. FROG (VI). Signed Limited Edition. Chuck
Jones, 1994. Discovered in a cornerstone laid many decades
past, the box is opened, Michigan J. Frog leaps out and
instantaneously bursts into song.

The Tasmanian Devil

Whirling and chewing through rocks and trees, terrifying wildlife, eating anything in sight but satisfied with only one specific kind of meal: rabbit. Meet the Tasmanian Devil.

Here's another character who achieved immortality after appearing in just a few films—only five between 1954 (*Devil May Hare*) and 1964 (*Dr. Devil and Mr. Hare*) all directed by Taz's creator, Robert McKimson. But the Tasmanian Devil was such a popular character that he didn't require any more footage to become an unforgettable entity. Indeed, Taz is the embodiment of raw primal power—a whirling, swirling mass of force; a miniature tornado with tiny legs and spindly, flailing arms.

The Tasmanian guidebook in the first film describes him as "a vicious, ravenous brute, with powerful jaws like a steel trap." The entry then proceeds to catalogue some of the luckless animals on the beast's menu (Taz himself adds rabbits to the list). Taz auteur Bob McKimson

TAZ MODEL SHEET. Limited Edition. Warner Bros., 1994. "Taz Boy" in a variety of devilish poses.

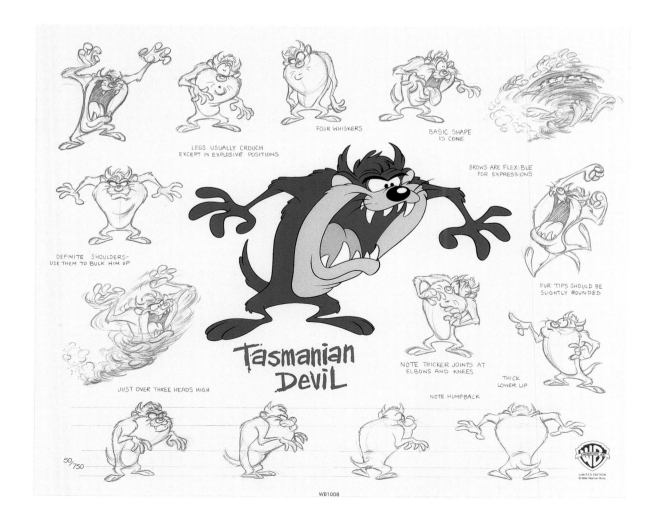

FOUR WHISKERS

LEGS USUALLY CROUCH EXCEPT IN EXPLOSIVE POSITIONS

BASIC SHAPE IS CONE

BROWS ARE FLEXIBLE FOR EXPRESSIONS

DEFINITE SHOULDERS- USE THEM TO BULK HIM UP

FUR TIPS SHOULD BE SLIGHTLY ROUNDED

Tasmanian Devil

NOTE THICKER JOINTS AT ELBOWS AND KNEES

THICK LOWER LIP

JUST OVER THREE HEADS HIGH

NOTE HUMPBACK

50/750

WB1008

recalled that the character was born when writer Sid Marcus was "kicking around different types of characters. And I said, 'About the only thing we haven't used around here is a Tasmanian Devil.' He didn't even know what they were. And we just started talking about it and we came up with this character." However, "Taz Boy" was almost stillborn when, after that first episode, cartoon producer Edward Selzer deemed him too gruesome. Taz was finally revived three years later at the behest of studio head Jack Warner himself, who was irritated that the character had been retired after one cartoon.

In later films, the Tasmanian Devil continued to battle Bugs Bunny (and, in the memorable *Ducking the Devil*, Daffy Duck). Like Bugs's other sparring partners, Taz proves susceptible to Bugs in drag (disguised as a "she-devil"—with a lip-sticked bear trap in his kisser—in *Bedevilled Rabbit*), but any similarity to Elmer or Yosemite Sam ends there. It's no surprise that youngsters and teenagers would latch onto him, since Taz's explosive energy and aggression can be viewed as a metaphor for the frustrating condition known as "growing up."

(*Top*) TAZ AND BRIDE (II). Signed Limited Edition. Friz Freleng, 1989. Bugs administers the vows in a Freleng scene inspired by Bob McKimson's *Devil May Hare* (1954). The 1992 TV series "Taz-Mania" was inspired by these classic cartoons.

(*Above*) LOOK, NO MEAT! Limited Edition. Robert McKimson, 1991. Bugs tries to convince the Tasmanian Devil that he's not worth eating in this scene inspired by his enduring series of Taz cartoons.

(*Left*) TAZ RIPPED. Limited Edition. Robert McKimson, signed by his brother, Warner Bros. animator Tom McKimson, 1992. Bad call? Taz is literally chewing up the bases in this McKimson limited-edition scene.

(*Opposite*) CLASSIC TAZ. Limited Edition. Robert McKimson, 1989. Classic Taz: Thumbs up for the Devil, in a typical woodland setting, as in his 1962 entry, McKimson's *Bill Of Hare*, the latter title being a reference to our anti-hero's infamously devilish appetite.

AP/500

© Warner Bros. Inc. 1989

Speedy Gonzales

He arrived with his usual lusty cry of "Andale! Andale!" (followed by "Arriba! Arriba!" with an "eh-hah!" thrown in as a capper) in Robert McKimson's 1953 *Cat-Tails for Two*, but otherwise, the rodent was unrecognizable as the Speedy audiences know today. After the premiere episode, the studio decided that the gangly, gold-toothed mouse could stand some cutening—which is what he received, courtesy of Friz Freleng and co-designer Hawley Pratt, in his second appearance, Freleng's *Speedy Gonzales*. The makeover was so successful that the mouse and the cartoon bagged an Academy Award. In 1957, Speedy (via McKimson) was nominated again for *Tabasco Road*.

Chalk it up to virtuosity that Warner was the first studio to specialize in multiculturalism. With Mel Blanc's help, the Warner cartoonists could more easily present such examples of cultural diversity as the French Pepé Le Pew, the Southern-fried Foghorn Leghorn, and the Brooklynite Bugs Bunny. A Hispanic cartoon star (the voice in some ways an outgrowth of Mel Blanc's "Sy" the Mexican on "The Jack Benny Show") was only natural.

Friz Freleng's *Speedy Gonzales* inducted Sylvester, the studio's long-suffering Everycat, into yet another series. His efforts to catch "the fastest mouse in all Mehico" were just as fruitless—and as funny—as his pursuits of Tweety and Hippety Hopper. Although Sylvester and Speedy were a team that could do no wrong (as in such efforts as *Gonzales' Tamales*), Freleng teamed Speedy with other predators as well, such as the bird-brained buzzard "El Vulturo" (in *Tortilla Flaps*) and the dimwitted Chicano cats known as the Mexicali Shmoes. In the 1960s, the ever-grousing Daffy Duck traveled south of the border to make after the mouse. Speedy was forever escaping these king-sized troublemakers, not only with his speed, but with his wits, charisma, and eternal optimism.

MEXICAN CAT DANCE. Limited Edition. Friz Freleng, 1995. The fastest mouse in all Mexico and El Gato are, for once, making music rather than mayhem, as Freleng usually had them doing. Sylvester clanks his cat-stenets as he does a cat hat dance around a convenient sombrero, while Speedy supplies a Latin downbeat.

Pepé Le Pew

More than any other Warner star, Chuck Jones's Pepé Le Pew is a creature of irony—he knows himself to be a great lover, but he can never get up close and personal with *l'objects du affecion* because they are immediately repulsed by his skunk's scent. A further irony is that Pepé never realizes that these *petite femme skunks fatale* are not skunks at all but rather *les pussycats* who somehow happen to have white stripes painted down their backs. But does this perpetual state of interruptus leave our odorous Casanova, to say the least, frustrated? Not on your little pink tomato nose! Pepé is so unshakable in his libidinous confidence that nothing, but nothing, can deter him; he continually presses on in his pursuit of *femme chats* across the Gallic landscape.

Charles Boyer, the transplanted French romantic leading man, was a film icon long before his most famous role as "Pepé Le Moko" in the 1938 film *Algiers*. With the aid of Mel Blanc's capacity for accents and

PEPÉ LE PEW MODEL SHEET. Limited Edition. Warner Bros., 1996. Animation's greatest *loveur par excellence*, seen here in a variety of poses *romantique*, each one calculated to make a female skunk fall head over heels for this handsome hunk of skunk.

CARROTBLANCA. Limited Edition. Warner Bros. Classic
Animation, 1995. Jealousy isn't the only thing in the air as
Sylvester watches his love interest get swept up by Constable
Le Pew in this limited-edition scene from the cartoon.

imitations, Pepé Le Pew brings to mind the romantic Boyer. It was evident in the skunk's first appearance, 1945's *Odor-able Kitty*, that the character had potential. Then, after bagging the Oscar for their fourth Pepé picture, *For Scent-imental Reasons* (1949), director Chuck Jones and writer Michael Maltese realized that here indeed was *un star du cinema!*

Jones and Maltese continued to turn out an *epic du Pepé* almost every year until 1962. Later entries bring the stink-crossed lovers not only out on the boulevards of Paris but across the French-speaking world, to such locales as France's most famous art museum (*Louvre Come Back to Me!*), a Foreign Legion outpost (*Little Beau Pepé*), the French Alps (*A Scent of the Matterhorn*), and once even back to the original Casbah in Algiers (*The Cats Bah*, 1954), where the whole Pepé mystique began. "Just theenk, radiant flower," Pepé coos in this 1954 gem, "you do not have to come with me to ze Casbah—we are already here!"

Oui-oui, Le Pew.

(*Below*) SOMETHEENG? Signed Limited Edition. Chuck Jones, 1983. We all knew that Pepé's pungency not only stops all females dead in their tracks, but here's proof positive that even male antagonists find Pepé's odoriferous personality positively arresting.

(*Opposite, top*) PEPÉ'S 50TH BIRTHDAY. Signed Limited Edition. Chuck Jones, 1995. For Pepé's big 50th birthday, old friend Bugs had to serve him his cake and candles via a cake plate with a ten-foot handle—and you'll note that the other Looney Tunes cast members stood so far back that they weren't even in camera range!

(*Opposite, left*) SHE IS SHY. Signed Limited Edition. Chuck Jones, 1993. Pepé mistakes the wet paint down *la femme pussycat's* back for a skunk's stripe, and gives chase, not realizing he's actually instigating an out-of-species relationship. *Ooh-la la! Embrasse moi!*

(*Opposite, right*) ROMEO AND JULIET. Signed Limited Edition. Chuck Jones, 1992. The skunk invokes Shakespeare's greatest lover in a characteristically fragrant treatment of *Romeo and Juliet's* balcony scene.

LE PURSUIT. Signed Limited Edition. (Diptych, *this page and opposite*). Chuck Jones, 1994. As eager as he is to start *"ze l'amour"* (not to mention *"ze toujour!"*), Pepé never rushes. By keeping an even, steady pace, he knows the objects of his desire will be in his arms, sooner or later.

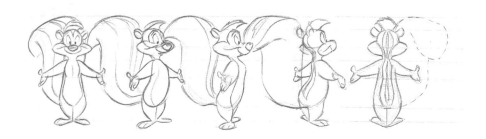

His heart's desire: *"Une Petite Femme Skunk Fatale,"*
invariably a female cat who haplessly wandered under a
freshly painted white ladder.

The Road Runner & Wile E. Coyote

Nearly all of Chuck Jones's two dozen Road Runner pictures open with the parallel protagonists freeze-framed and identified in ersatz-Latin terms such as "Speedibus rex" and "Famishus famishus." This helps us to think of the Road Runner and Coyote not so much as characters but as raw elemental forces: the first pure speed, the second pure desperation. The exclusively formulaic nature of the cartoons also contributes to that conclusion, each episode (which all take place in the same desert setting) consisting of a dozen or so gags in which the Coyote tries to catch his speedy prey with increasingly elaborate contraptions that invariably backfire on him.

Yet the Road Runner and Coyote are cinematic personalities of the highest order. The pursuer, eventually identified (and given a voice in his battles with Bugs Bunny) as Wile E. Coyote, may be frustration personified, but he's clearly flesh and blood. We feel for him when boulders flatten him, when the TNT goes off two seconds too soon, when he plummets from a cliff of almost incomprehensible height, only to have his pain trivialized, in our eyesight, to a tiny puff of desert dust. The Road Runner, too, is far from simply a "beep-beep"-ing straight man to the Coyote's self-defeating machinations. While the Bird generally speeds by oblivious to Wile E.'s schemes to do him in, he's not above revelling in his own apparent invulnerability. For instance, when the Coyote's phony railroad setup produces a real locomotive at the end of *Beep, Beep* (1952), the Road Runner is delighted to be sitting pretty in the engine as it tramples the hapless schemer.

The genesis of the Road Runner and Coyote films came from several sources, not the least of which was Jones's desire to climax the studio's "hunting" fixation with the ultimate chase format. Then too, since boyhood the director had been fascinated by Mark Twain's description of the coyote as "a long, slim, sick and sorry-looking skeleton with a gray wolfskin stretched over it . . . With a despairing eye of forsakenness and misery . . . The coyote is a living and breathing allegory of Want. He is always poor, out of luck, and friendless." The team was introduced in 1949's *Fast And Furry-ous*. The series grew leaner and meaner until Jones's departure in 1964, with writer Maltese's gags becoming as trimly economic as Maurice Noble's increasingly stylized settings (Noble also went on to direct Wile E./Road Runner shorts, as did Rudy Larriva, Bob McKimson, and Abe Levitow). Through it all, Jones, as he has often said, was inspired by a dictum of another great American philosopher, George Santayana, who observed, "A fanatic is someone who redoubles his effort when he has forgotten his aim."

(Above) ROAD RUNNER CLASSIC (II). Signed Limited Edition. Chuck Jones, 1989. The joy of "beep, beep!" A rare shot of *Velocitus tremendus* just as he takes that oh-so-slight leap in the air before *Zipping Along*.

(Opposite) TURNABOUT IS FAIR PLAY. Signed Limited Edition. Chuck Jones, 1993. A further demonstration of the remarkable velocity achieved by the *Desert baduouticus*: he runs so fast he not only makes our heads spin, but he succeeds in quite literally tying the body of *Hardheadipus delirius* into knots.

396/750

50150

©1993 Warner Bros.

(*Left*) ACME HARPOON GUN. Signed Limited Edition. Chuck Jones, 1994. (*Below*) SKIING. Signed Limited Edition. Chuck Jones, 1989. The rarest of all shots—*Tastyus supersonicus* and *Eternali famishiis* shown in hot pursuit, as ever, but just this once, running where no road is in sight. From the team's 1979 reunion effort, *Freeze Frame*.

(*Opposite, top*) HIGH STRUNG COYOTE. Signed Limited Edition. Chuck Jones, 1986. Another variation on the arrow idea, this time from *Guided Muscle* (1955).

(*Opposite, bottom*) ACME BIRD SEED. Signed Limited Edition. Chuck Jones, 1993. *Zipping* right *Along*, here we come to an instance when *Famishus famishus* tries booby trapping some bird seed left for *Speedibus rex* with iron pellets. It should be foolproof—the iron in the Bird's stomach attracts a magnet pulling the Coyote, yet he somehow manages to wind up pinned to an explosive just the same.

(*Above*) ACME BATMAN. Signed Limited Edition. Chuck
Jones, 1991. Well, *Gee Whiz-z-z-z-z-z*. Here's a valuable
document of *Eatibus almost anythingus* in one of his most
outlandish attempts yet at trapping *Velocitus delictibus*, this
time donning the disguise known as the "Acme
Bat-man's outfit." As a commercial pitchman guarantees in
Jones's featurette *The Adventures of the Road Runner*, this is
"the only Batman outfit worn by real bats!"

(*Opposite*) SUSPENDED ANIMATION. Signed Limited
Edition. Chuck Jones, 1994. It's all in a day's work: The Road
Runner and Coyote pictures establish their twin protagonists
as elemental entities. But in shorts starring "Ralph Wolf"
opposite the visually impaired but eternally resourceful "Sam
Sheepdog," the character of Ralph emphasizes both his
humanity and his professionalism in the face of what Bugs
Bunny would term "serious hoit."

125/750

© 1994 Warner Bros

Foghorn Leghorn

Characters based on film and radio stars proliferated at Warners, but usually in one-shot appearances (thus allowing Daffy to be pursued by Victor Moore in Friz Freleng's *Ain't That Ducky* [1945] and Peter Lorre in Robert McKimson's *Birth of a Notion* [1947]). However, a fast-talking, blustery confederate rooster (created and directed by Bob McKimson) represented the only major recurring character (apart from Pepé Le Pew) to be inspired by an extra-studio source. Veteran announcer and actor Kenny Delmar portrayed the loudmouthed "Senator Claghorn from Bighorn" for many seasons on Fred Allen's "Allen's Alley." Long before the character became "Foghorn" (meaning loud) "Leghorn" (a subspecies of chicken), Delmar's expressions like "That's a joke, son!" had been national catchphrases.

As it happened, Mel Blanc could do the Claghorn/Foghorn voice even better than its originator, as he proved in the first Foggy film, *Walky Talky Hawky*. As that 1946 title suggests, the rooster was originally intended as a foil for the diminutive and determined carnivore, Henery Hawk (whose histrionic father dramatically informs Henery that he was born to eat chicken, the major drawback being that Henery doesn't know what a chicken looks like). The big rooster almost immediately takes all the play away from the tiny chicken hawk, and by the next film, *Crowing Pains* (1947), Henery, still foraging for fowl, is clearly Foggy's foil.

Within a few films, Henery himself is usurped by the Barnyard Dawg (who turns up in one Porky Pig entry, 1947's *One Meat Brawl*, identified as "Mandrake") as Foghorn's main sparring partner. Foggy and doggy then spend most of seventeen cartoons trying to one-up the other. Foghorn has other encounters too, with Sylvester (*Crowing Pains*, 1947), Daffy Duck (*The High and the Flighty*, 1956), and Miss Prissy (most hysterically in *Of Rice And Hen*, 1953), both with and without her brilliant offspring Egghead Jr. (as in *Little Boy Boo*, 1954).

It should be noted that most of Foghorn's rustic free-for-alls were directed by the rooster's originator, Robert McKimson. In 1996, Chuck and Linda Jones produced and Darrell Van Citters directed *Pullet Surprise* which, coincidentally, pairs the big blowhard with another McKimson creation, the addle-brained Pete Puma. In recent years, the Classic Animation group has provided Foghorn's talents to TV specials, features, and commercials. And throughout it all, Foghorn Leghorn practically never stops talking. Talking, that is.

(Opposite, top) LET'S PLAY CROQUET. Limited Edition. Robert McKimson (facsimile signature), 1991. Foghorn's not exactly a team player here, an image inspired by more than a dozen Foghorn Leghorn cartoons in which he acts out revenge on the Barnyard Dawg.

(Opposite, bottom) NO SPRING CHICKEN. Signed Limited Edition. Friz Freleng, 1994. When it comes to matters of love, Foghorn's got a lot to learn, although anything is music to Miss Prissy's ears.

"AH SAY -- TAKE IT PRISSY.
AT THE PACE YOU'RE GOIN' IT'LL
TAKE YOU FIFTY YEARS TO GET A BOUQUET
-- AND YOU'RE RUNIN' OUT A TIME."

Marvin The Martian

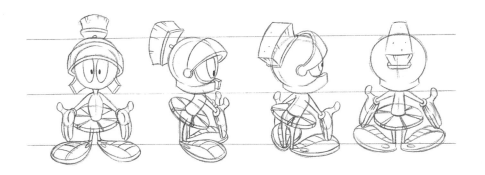

As Looney Tunes entered the space age, it was only natural that Bugs Bunny should encounter an off-world foil, a "heavy" not of this Earth. Marvin's costume, patterned on the ancient Roman depiction of the god Mars, is as warlike as his ray-gun, but his voice and disposition are more nebbishy than the most timid bookkeeper. Over the course of several classic Chuck Jones cartoons, the Martian would attempt to incinerate Bugs (or, in one case, Daffy) and blow up the Earth in the process ("It blocks my view of Venus," he observes petulantly).

Certainly the studio never went farther afield for a second banana for Bugs Bunny: in the first space opera, *Haredevil Hare* (1948), the rabbit is coaxed into taking an experimental rocket voyage by scientists who stuff their vehicle full of carrots. (In this early episode, man and Martian

MARVIN THE MARTIAN MODEL SHEET. Limited Edition. Warner Bros., 1995. The many faces of the little creature with no face.

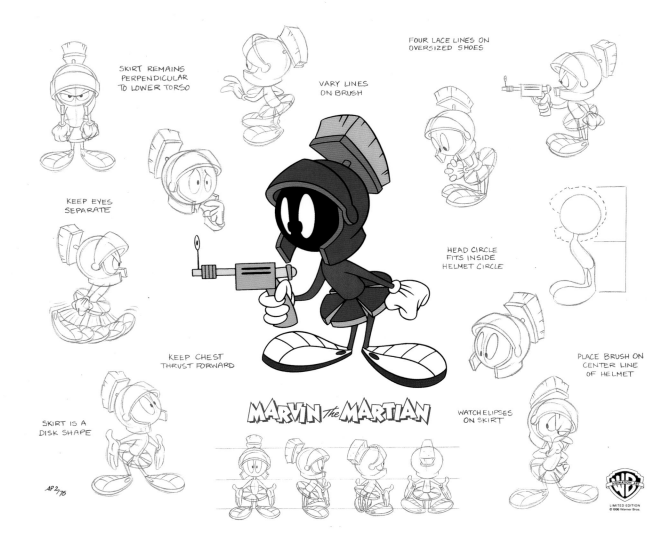

AP 2/50

LIMITED EDITION
© 1996 Warner Bros.

You Can't Escape Me, Dodgers! Limited Edition.
Created by Warner Bros. Classic Animation, 1996. Marvin
and Daffy return to the big screen in the state-of-the-art 3-D
short *Marvin The Martian In The 3rd Dimension*, from which
this image is culled, in which Marvin mistakes Daffy's cheapo
space movie to be a genuine intergalactic threat.

do battle not with futuristic weapons but with old-fashioned cartoon dynamite.) *The Hasty Hare* (1952), the second appearance of Marvin and his green Martian mutt (ever-faithful Lt. K-9), finds the two aliens coming to Earth in an attempt to haul Bugs back with them as a lab specimen. The Martian's *pièce de résistance*, however, may be *Duck Dodgers in the 24 1/2th Century* (1953), a Flash Gordon parody in which the "thing from another world" battles Daffy Duck over the universe's major source of "Illudium Phosdex" ("the shaving cream atom").

Later adventures are even more surreal. *Hare-Way To The Stars* (1958) has Bugs accidentally hauled off to outer space and playing tag with Marvin across a futuristic cityscape of transparent panels hanging in emptiness (a *tour de force* for designer Maurice Noble). *Mad As A Mars Hare* (1963) has the rabbit rocketing to Marvin's home planet and, in a turnaround windup, is de-evolutionized into a monstrous brute of a Neanderthal hare.

The Marvin of the 1990s had a most apropos cameo role in *Space Jam*, and stars (with Daffy Duck) in a breakthrough film, *Marvin The Martian in the 3rd Dimension*, a 13-minute, 70mm, CGI-animated, 3-D tour de force directed by Douglas McCarthy and produced by Kathleen Helppie-Shipley and Mark Eades. Marvin has become a star, a classic "villain we love to hate." And despite his warlike ways and his relentless ambition to obliterate terra firma, it's hard to think of this mouthless wonder, this ebony inkblot, as a true villain. After all, how can one hate an interplanetary entity who's always warbling, "Hmmm . . . Isn't that *lovely?*"

(Below, left) METER LEADER. Signed Limited Edition. Chuck Jones, 1995. Marvin The Martian assumes that Earthlings must somehow look like him. Silly, isn't he?

(Below, right) PEACE AND CARROTS. Signed Limited Edition. Chuck Jones, 1994. Marvin lands on Earth and, not knowing how to get to Roswell, New Mexico (Bugs himself has a hard time with Albuquerque), finds himself on the Rabbit's doorstep. The Rabbit, naturally, does not stand still for this attempted alien abduction or even a close encounter of any kind.

INSTANT MARTIANS. Signed Limited Edition. Chuck Jones, 1995. Marvin and his vulture-ostrich–like "Instant Martians" (who also gave Sylvester, though not Porky Pig, the scare of his life in *Jumpin' Jupiter*.) prepare to obliterate Earth. To create these ready-to-wear aliens, all one need do is add water to a pill, but it looks like the midget Martian on the left could stand another drop or two in this cel inspired by Chuck Jones's *Hare-way To The Stars*.

TINY TOONS

ANIMANIACS

PINKY AND THE BRAIN

BATMAN

SUPERMAN

THE NEW NEW CARTOONS

Tiny Toons

When the time comes for creating a chronology of the second "Golden Age" of Warner Bros. Animation, the year 1990 will certainly be the starting point. As the final decade of the century opened, a new crop of fertile minds added an entirely new generation of animated stars to the Warner menagerie, engaging and delighting a modern audience in their own language, and on their home turf: television.

The show was "Steven Spielberg Presents Tiny Toon Adventures." And with no less than Spielberg's name above the title, the fuse for an explosion of creative energy was lit by Jean MacCurdy and Tom Ruegger, whose extensive animation industry credits guaranteed able hands for such a high-profile endeavor.

Spielberg had come to Warner Bros. in 1988 with an idea for a feature-length animated film. While the film never came to fruition, a television project did. TV animation leader MacCurdy quickly hired Ruegger to produce the show and pull together a creative team.

(Previous spread) INSIDE THE WATERTOWER. Limited Edition. Warner Bros., 1994. Home of the Warner Bros. Yakko and Wakko (and the Warner Sister, Dot!).

(Below) TINY TOONS LINE-UP. Sericel. Warner Bros., 1991. The cast of "Steven Spielberg Presents Tiny Toon Adventures" ushered in Warners' seventh decade in animation.

Within two weeks, Ruegger and his hand-picked group had pieced
together the show's concept, its characters, and a series "bible." By April,
Spielberg had approved several completed scripts for the Tiny Toon
"shorts." The show was on its way.

Ruegger's vision from the outset was to "recapture the magic of the
Warner Bros. Looney Tunes with new characters." In the show, the
Tiny Toons' mentors would be the Looney Tunes themselves who would
show the brash young upstarts how to live and cope in a cartoon world.
The series creators adopted the same stance, rejecting many of the
established traditions of television cartoons.

"Tiny Toon Adventures" would be an unusual potpourri of short
cartoon segments, spot gags, and character schtick aimed at distinguishing
itself from the past while simultaneously paying it tribute.

Buster and Babs Bunny, Hamton Pig, Plucky Duck, Montana Max,
and Elmyra, on their home turf of Acme Acres and Acme Looniversity
(a sort of "Fame" campus for toons), carry on antics as spirited as those of
of the earlier Warner Bros. cartoon stars, but were geared to a somewhat
younger audience. What remained constant was the irreverent tone of the
original cartoons, with mischief and silliness tailor-made for 1990s kids.

370/950

Spielberg insisted on high production values, and Warner Bros. delivered in every area. While the writers—including Ruegger, Sherri Stoner, Wayne Kaatz, Paul Dini, and Tom Minton—created the funny scripts for the new character group, the animation "unit" system was reestablished at Warner Bros., with key directors Art Vitello, Rich Arons, Ken Boyer, Alfred Gimeno, and others leading their own teams of artists into the thick of production.

Voice director Andrea Romano assembled an amazing vocal cast (including Tress MacNeille, Charlie Adler, Don Messick, Joe Alaskey, Cree Summer, Maurice LaMarche, and Frank Welker). Bruce Broughton, the series' musical director, brought in many of the best composers in the industry—Fred Steiner, Mort Stevens, and Richard Stone, for example— to score the show.

"Tiny Toon Adventures" instantly grabbed a huge audience, winning Emmys for Outstanding Animated Program, Music Direction, and Original Song in its first season. "Tiny Toons" would go on to win four more Emmys and an Environmental Media Award.

But the awards and ratings were simply acknowledgment of what Spielberg, Ruegger, and MacCurdy knew all along: create a kids' show with imagination, energy, and attitude and audiences will scramble for it.

TINY TOONS WESTERN. Sericel. Created by Warner Bros. Classic Animation, 1993. Like the original Looney Tunes, Tiny Toons took place in many different locations and time periods.

Animaniacs

After the phenomenal ratings success of "Tiny Toon Adventures," Steven Spielberg, Tom Ruegger, and Jean MacCurdy were in the delightfully uncomfortable spot of having to follow up a "hit." "We all wanted to try something new," Ruegger recalled, "but there was reticence to launch another comedy series without a 'marquee name' involved."

Ruegger had come up with a concept inspired by the "unstoppable" energy of his three children, but Spielberg thought the characters—three little blue ducks—"had been done before." With the characters still in his head and the notion of a marquee name to put the series over, Ruegger had a "cartoon epiphany" one day on the Warner Bros. backlot as his eyes settled on the studio's landmark water tower, with its big, bold "WB" shield logo. "There was the marquee name," he explained, "'the Warner Brothers.' Their sister, Dot, soon followed."

OF MICE AND MANIACS. Sericel. Warner Bros., 1995. The Brain doesn't suffer fools gladly, but oh, does he suffer.

The show was called "Steven Spielberg Presents Animaniacs," and the three blue ducks became the Warner Brothers ("and the Warner Sister"). They were cartoon children (curiously, neither human nor animal), drawn in a style reminiscent of the black-and-white cartoon stars of the 1930s.

Ruegger and producers Rich Arons and Sherri Stoner purport that the Warners (Yakko, the talkative, Groucho-like one; Wakko, the voracious, Harpo-like one; and Dot, "the CUTE one!") were conceived decades earlier by the studio's most disturbed cartoonist, and were so uncontrollable that they had to be locked in the water tower to protect an unwary public. One day they escaped, and the chaos they created is the inspiration for the show. Design throwbacks as they were, they were pure 1990s creations, embodying the synthesis of old and new that was taking clearer shape as Warner cartoons moved further into their second epoch.

Each half-hour "Animaniacs" episode is a breakneck compilation of segments assembled much like "Tiny Toon Adventures," except with the humor level ratcheted up several notches. Seemingly every moment contains some kind of wisecrack, pun (both verbal and visual), or slapstick gag—sometimes simultaneously—all the while driving the loosest of stories. "Animaniacs" pokes ungoverned, sharp-edged fun at a world that seems, even to adults, completely out of control. The Animaniacs characters don't fight the world, they spin with it, the writers slapping hilariously irreverent commentary into the scripts like cultural flypaper. And the Warner Brothers, with their clever (and brutal) defiance of authority and conformity, are champions for children.

Ruegger and company have made it clear that nothing is sacred to the show, certainly a nod to the earlier generation of Looney Tunes writers and artists who fought the insanity of a warring, demoralized, industrialized world by laughing at it. And added to the Animaniacs mix is a company of lower-echelon Mafia pigeons (Goodfeathers), an over-the-hill cartoon squirrel (voiced by series co-producer Stoner) who gets back into the business to battle the blandness (and political correctness) of modern cartoons, and a pair of laboratory mice with dreams of taking over the world. The universe is filled out with a gallery of supporting psychiatrists, cops, nurses, teachers, and zany studio heads, held together by a mortar of wickedly clever musical segments that deal with history, geography, math, and every segment of modern culture (including devastatingly funny parodies of celebrities, movies, game shows, and the people who love them).

All of this is pulled off with rich and fluid animation and painstakingly detailed layout artwork the likes of which hasn't been seen in original television animation for decades.

When "Animaniacs" premiered in the fall of 1993, it was an even bigger hit than "Tiny Toons" had been three years earlier, and had a large adult fan base. The Warners team earned more Emmys, as well as the prestigious George Foster Peabody Award, and the show itself helped to set the tone for the fledgling Fox Network and drive up its ratings.

The chemistry of Spielberg and Ruegger's creative team that had put the "Tiny Toons" over the top propelled "Animaniacs" as well. The voice

(*Opposite*) STAR TRUCK. Limited Edition. Warner Bros. Classic Animation, 1996. Yakko, Wakko, and Dot prepare to beam supporting characters Pinky and the Brain into their own spin-off series.

HELLO NURSE. Limited Edition. Warner Bros. Classic Animation, 1995. The "Warner brothers." invade the office of Dr. Otto Scratchansniff, much to the confusion of Warner sister Dot and the beautiful "Hello Nurse."

cast, again assembled by Andrea Romano, featured the versatile Tress MacNeille, Rob Paulsen, and Jess Harnell (whose Beatle-esque, Liverpudlian stylings as Wakko were a series highlight), as well as Maurice LaMarche, who put a brilliant Orson Wellesian spin on The Brain. Richard Stone's rich scores, coupled with intelligently hilarious songs by Randy Rogel, filled out the show's distinctive sound, which has blossomed into three best-selling compact discs.

The work of series creator Ruegger and the talented team of writers (including Paul Rugg, Peter Hastings, Deanna Oliver, John McCann, Sherri Stoner, Tom Minton, and Nicholas Hollander) and segment directors (including Rich Arons, Rusty Mills, Alfred Gimeno, Jon McClenahan, and Gary Hartle) made the show so popular that one "Animaniacs" cartoon, *I'm Mad*, was actually given a theatrical release, thus following the classic animation Looney Tunes in a return to the big screen.

BALONEY IN OUR SLACKS. Limited Edition. Warner Bros. Classic Animation, 1996. The "Animaniacs" supporting cast look on as the "Warner Bros." (and sister, Dot) illustrate a line in their theme song depicting "bologna in our slacks."

Pinky and The Brain

*O*ne is a genius—the other's insane.

Before "Animaniacs" hit the middle of its first season, it was clear that children weren't the only ones who were hooked— adults were getting big laughs from the show's nervy slaps at cultural icons, trends, and pretensions. And who has more contempt for the pretensions of the culture than The Brain, whose revulsion at most of what he sees is overshadowed by his desire to rule it.

"Pinky and The Brain," and their world, which was again under the creative guidance of Tom Ruegger, hit a chord with the audience and with the creators themselves, who enjoyed flexing their creative muscles on a project geared more toward a grown-up audience. Ruegger, with writer/producer Peter Hastings, producer/directors Rusty Mills and Liz Holzman, and writers Charlie Howell and Gordon Bressack, created something that was wholly fresh and new, independent of the Looney Tunes legacy in every way except tone.

Pinky and The Brain are, as the main title theme song explains, "laboratory mice—their genes have been spliced," and in each episode, the scientifically altered rodents try to take over the world ("To prove their mousey worth—they'll overthrow the Earth").

Brain's egomaniacal schemes involved such appealingly ridiculous images as the tiny mouse operating from within a full-size human costume, the better to infiltrate the world of men he so desperately seeks to conquer. Brain is not a villain, nor is he mean; his desire to take over the world is fueled by his belief that the world would be a better place if he were in charge. Nor is Pinky a blithering idiot (all of the time). Sometimes he has accidental bursts of wisdom, the import of which escapes him.

Brain's put-downs of Pinky aren't cruel because we know Pinky doesn't quite understand them. Like Laurel and Hardy, whose humor certainly echoes here, Pinky and The Brain are pals—they'd be lost without each other.

Once the college-age crowd became hip to the duo, the series began a separate run as part of The WB's Sunday prime-time lineup. Maurice La Marche's obsessed, somber, Orson Wellesian interpretation of The Brain, and Rob Paulsen's manically dimwitted (but thoroughly charming) Pinky were vocal characterizations of the highest order. Directed by the omnipresent Andrea Romano, they contributed in no small measure to the series' success, as did Richard Stone's musical compositions.

Though their newest characters were innovative and unprecedented, Ruegger and his crew's love of vintage entertainment was still evident in

PINKY & THE BRAIN. Limited Edition. Warner Bros. Classic
Animation, 1995. "Pinky and The Brain" wasted no time in
taking over the TV animation world.

451/500

NO FREE CHEESE. Limited Edition. Warner Bros. Classic Animation, 1995. After making their debut on Steven Spielberg's "Animaniacs," Pinky and The Brain became break-out stars, eventually getting their own series—certainly a solid first step toward world domination.

the content of the cartoons. One of the early short cartoons, "Puppet Rulers" (story by Peter Hastings, written by Tom Minton, directed by Barry Caldwell and Dave Marshall), was a particularly clever take on pop culture's effect on the baby boom generation. In this marvelously conceived effort, Pinky and The Brain decide to become beloved puppet show characters of the 1950s, then travel via time machine into the future, where they attempt to exploit the nostalgic love that the generation—now grown-up—still has for them.

Although the overly ambitious mice never achieve their dictatorial goals, "Pinky and The Brain" did win a Prime-time Emmy in 1996 for Outstanding Animated Program, representing yet another triumph for Spielberg, Ruegger, MacCurdy, and Warner Bros. Television Animation with the emergence of a bright, new style in Warner Bros. cartoons.

Or, as Pinky would say it, "Egad! Narf!"

Pi(e). Limited Edition. Warner Bros. Classic Animation, 1996. So, that's what keeps them together—they both love pie!

Batman

Batman" publisher DC Comics had become a part of the Warner corporate family in 1968, and it was only natural that with the revitalization of the Warner Bros. animation unit, cartoons would come a-knockin' on DC's door. "Batman" was first to make the transition, not least because of the success of the 1989 Tim Burton feature. Burton himself was a consultant to the subsequent animated series, but the cartoon Caped Crusader went even further than his wide screen counterpart into a world where just about anything could happen (and usually did).

BATMAN MODEL SHEET. Limited Edition. Created by Warner Bros. Classic Animation and Warner Bros. Television Animation, 1996. This model sheet demonstrates the unprecedented visual dynamic of the "Batman" series.

I AM THE NIGHT. Limited Edition. Created by Warner
Bros. Television Animation, 1993. "Batman" took place
in a film noirish nightscape far removed from the perpetual
daylight of earlier adventure cartoons.

"Batman: The Animated Series" (later known as "The Adventures of Batman & Robin") was a complete departure for Warner Bros. Animation. Not only was it not meant to be funny, it was often downright gloomy. And that was its strength. "Batman" was a dark, morbid, surrealistic flight through a timeless netherworld where 1930s cars exist side by side with Art Deco cellular phones, and garish villains are met by the grim vigilante that is Batman himself. Many believe that "Batman" is the finest animated super hero series ever produced.

Several members of Jean MacCurdy and Tom Ruegger's "Tiny Toons"/"Animaniacs" creative team became the movers and shakers behind the program, with Ruegger himself (and writer-producer Paul Dini) writing the series "bible." Bruce Timm and Eric Radomski, who had, respectively, designed characters and backgrounds for "Tiny Toons" and "Animaniacs," produced a two-minute test film which set the tone and look of the show. Timm, Radomski, and Alan Burnett, along with Ruegger and MacCurdy, became executive producers of "Batman, the Animated Series," with Ruegger, Timm, Dini, and Randy Rogel creating scripts dealing with themes seldom touched upon by animated TV shows. The writing and animation struck a chord with audiences (and discriminating Batman fans), making the show a hit that went on to win several Emmys.

Dini believes the definitive "Batman" episode was "Heart of Ice," which featured a new take on the origin of Batman's classic adversary, Mr. Freeze. In the episode, the villain, at first a cryogenics expert named Victor Fries, was acting out of grief over the death of his beloved wife. "It just showed a lot of the elements of Batman that we really wanted to concentrate on," explains Dini. "It showed Batman as a grim and quiet character. It had a surprisingly touching and human story amid the action." The episode, written by Dini and directed by Timm, won an Emmy for best writing.

Perhaps more notably, the series—in part spawned by the live-action *Batman* films—itself spawned a theatrical feature, *Batman: Mask of the Phantasm*. Though Warner Bros. Cartoons had produced cartoon segments of the features *Two Guys From Texas*, *My Dream Is Yours*, and *The Incredible Mr. Limpett* and had produced compilation features like *Daffy Duck's Movie: Fantastic Island*, its cartoon division had never before produced a full-length theatrical film. In every respect, "Batman" took Warner Bros. Animation where it had never gone before.

HEART OF ICE. Limited Edition. Warner Bros. Television Animation, 1995. Batman encounters the cold-blooded Mr. Freeze.

(*Opposite, top*) BE A CLOWN. Limited Edition. Warner Bros. Television Animation, 1993. Sherlock Holmes had Moriarty; Batman has the Joker.

(*Opposite, bottom*) MARK OF A QUESTION. Limited Edition. Warner Bros. Television Animation, 1995. The Riddler tries to rid Gotham of Batman.

BATMAN VILLAIN LINE-UP. Sericel. Created by Warner Bros. Television Animation, 1994. The series drew from one of the greatest Rogues Galleries in the history of comics: Mr. Freeze, Poison Ivy, Penguin, Joker, Harley Quinn, Mad Hatter, Riddler, Catwoman, and Two-Face.

DYNAMIC DUO. Limited Edition. Created by Warner Bros. Television Animation, 1996. The Dynamic Duo respond to the Bat-Signal.

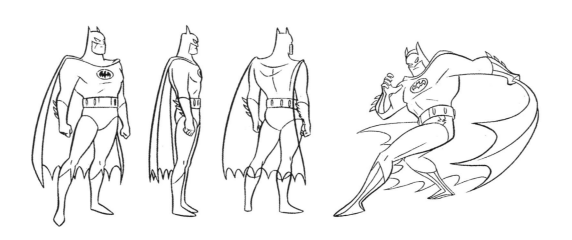

HARLEY TOYS WITH BATMAN. Limited Edition. Created by Warner Bros. Television Animation, 1994. Harley Quinn uses a classic cartoon prop, a mallet, to oppose Batman.

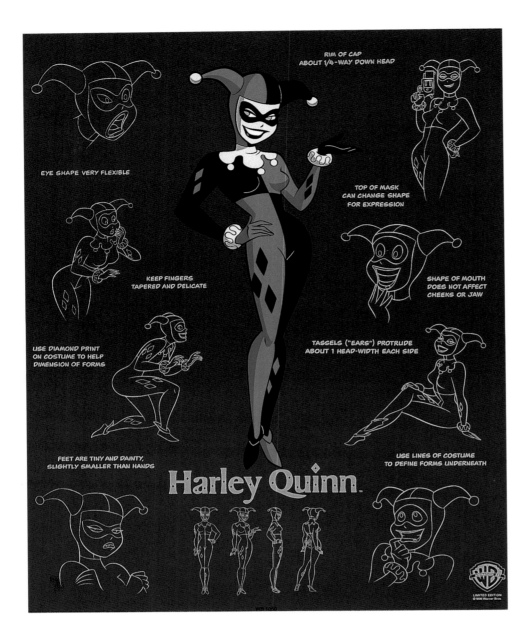

The women in Batman's life:
(Left) HARLEY QUINN MODEL SHEET. Limited Edition.
Created by Warner Bros. Television Animation, 1995.

(Below) WHEN BAT'S AWAY, THE GIRLS WILL PLAY.
Limited Edition. Created by Warner Bros. Television
Animation, 1996. Batgirl and Catwoman.

(Opposite) THE CAT AND THE CLAW. Limited Edition.
Created by Warner Bros. Television Animation, 1993.
Is it love or hate? Catwoman vs. Batman.

(*Above*) ALMOST GOT 'IM. Limited Edition. Created by Warner Bros. Classic Animation, 1995. The Joker's wild—and the other four are insane.

(*Left*) GIRLS' NIGHT OUT. Limited Edition. Created by Warner Bros. Television Animation, 1996. The "Thelma and Louise" of Gotham City: Harley Quinn and Poison Ivy.

A TOUCH OF POISON IVY. Limited Edition. Created by
Warner Bros. Television Animation, 1994. Batman
suffers a bad case of Poison Ivy.

Superman

"Look! Up in the sky!"

"Superman," the follow-up to Warner's groundbreaking "Batman: The Animated Series," had a tough act to follow. With "Batman" having set a new standard in super hero animation, "Superman" stood little chance of making a similar impact. But trends in the world of super heroes are cyclical. For almost sixty years, Batman has had runs of tremendous popularity, then Superman takes over for awhile as America's favorite, then Batman again—around and around like a Viennese waltz. Just as the first Batman movie had been preceded by Frank Miller's "Dark Knight" comic book, then succeeded by the animated series, so had Superman been in the midst of a periodic resurgence when the new series came into being. The unprecedented death and reinterpretation of the character in the comic books had caught the fancy of public and media alike, and the "Lois & Clark" live-action series had become a bona fide hit. It was time for a new animated incarnation of the first of all super heroes.

The gang over at Warner Bros. Television Animation were more than ready to meet the challenge and show the world that "Batman" had not been a fluke. They knew that all super heroes were not alike and that "Superman" would both mandate and allow a different kind of storytelling than that to which they and the public had become accustomed. "Superman" is a "much different show from 'Batman,'" says producer Paul Dini, who with writer/producer Alan Burnett wrote the original proposal for the show as well as its 90-minute pilot episode. "The look is lighter and more colorful, but in many ways the characters are more complex," Dini explained.

If "Batman" had taken place in a somber, Deco world, then "Superman" would inhabit the bright optimism of the Streamline Moderne cityscape that is Metropolis. Art director Glen Murakami and character designer Shane Glines created for "Superman" the city New York had always hoped it would be—and a host of timeless denizens.

Paul Dini asserts that the best of the early episodes is "the one we did for prime time ('Last Son of Krypton'). It was a chance to tell the original story of 'Superman' in a way that it had never been visualized before," he went on to explain. "We also explored the trauma and joy of becoming a superhero in a way that had never been done before in the Superman mythos."

Dana Delany as Lois Lane and Tim Daly as the Man of Steel head the talented voice cast. Directors Dan Riba and Curt Geda are additional creative stalwarts. The series has carved out its own territory in the realm of Warner Bros. cartoon adventure, and there's no telling what single bounds the animation department will attempt next.

(Opposite) THE MAN OF STEEL. Limited Edition. Created by Warner Bros. Television Animation, 1996. Truth, Justice, and the American Way: The streamlined design of Superman (1996).

THE ART

Ruth Clampett on Animation Art

Although most animation fans are familiar with my father Bob Clampett's work, they may not realize that he was one of the first collectors of animation art. From his first animation at Warner Bros. to the countless drawings and cels he accumulated over the years, my father saved the art, not because he foresaw its future value, but because he loved it so much.

In addition to his own work, Dad also collected other animation art he admired, such as Winsor McCay's *Gertie the Dinosaur* and Tex Avery's work at MGM. For most of my childhood the vintage art remained tucked away while my brother, sister, and I painted with cel vinyl on acetate scraps or played with reject "Beany and Cecil" cels. Years later, my father lectured at colleges on the history of animation. To accompany his lecture, he and my mother, Sody, put together a traveling art exhibit that featured vintage cels, drawings, and model sheets. If he could have only known that years later this art would be hanging in New York's Museum of Modern Art! Certainly Dad's passion for animation art provided the inspiration that fuels my own animation art career.

As a tribute to Dad, my mother established in 1984 The Bob Clampett Animation Foundation to award scholarships to animation students. To raise money for the foundation, Mom decided we should sell limited-edition animation cels derived from my father's original animation. Linda Jones, daughter of Chuck Jones, had already established the limited-edition animation market in the late 1970s, and later Friz Freleng began producing editions from his Warner Bros. cartoons. The demand for this work grew because virtually all the original cels from the "Golden Age" of Warner Bros. cartoons had been destroyed. If someone wanted to own a classic scene with a background from a favorite Looney Tune, limited editions were available, and to this day remain affordable simply because they are less expensive than original production cels of the same period. Collectors appreciate that these great character scenes from memorable WB cartoons can be acquired, since they no longer exist in original production cels and backgrounds. Bob Clampett Animation Art was the first of the WB group to offer these unsigned limited editions from classic scenes.

Bob Clampett Animation Art was truly a family business, beginning with my sister, Cheri, my sister-in-law, Keiko, and I painting the cels. In the eight years Bob Clampett Animation Art existed, I watched the animation art business expand from one dealing in curious collectibles to a serious endeavor involving art galleries in every major city.

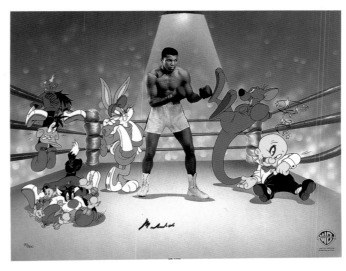

THE GREATEST. Limited Edition. Warner Bros., 1996.

(*Previous spread*) CHORUS LINE. Limited Edition. Warner Bros., 1990. (*Chapter title flap*) from THE GREAT SPACE ERASE. Limited Edition. Created by Warner Bros. Classic Animation, 1995.

ANTICIPATION. Signed Limited Edition. Friz Freleng, 1992. Spike and Chester have found a new plaything: Sylvester. Poor kitty. Inspired by Freleng's hilarious 1952 cartoon, *Tree For Two*.

In 1992, Warner Bros. established a new Animation Art Division. I was brought on by its director, Steve Felton, to oversee the creation and development of all limited-edition cels and sericels. When Warner Bros. first opened their Studio Stores in 1991, they had the foresight to feature a gallery-within-the-store concept. These Studio Store Galleries have since offered traditional animation art as well as sculpture, commissioned and print art, and gift collectibles. Warner Bros. Animation Art also distributes to an exclusive group of authorized independent galleries. Limited editions are a significant presence in both these venues.

While the purchase of a production cel is an opportunity to own an actual moment of a cartoon, a limited edition is a hand-painted tribute to the cartoon itself. Although I appreciate the "one-of-a-kind" aspect of production cels, great production cels are rare and can be expensive. With many of them, I notice unresolved poses with characters framed floating on a white-paper-background void. After all, production art was created to sit for a fraction of a second in front of a camera, not to hang framed on a wall. Limited editions (more often than not), because they are specially selected, achieve the perfect poses some production cels are unable to represent. After ten years of producing limited editions, I love the art form more than ever. The classic poses, matched with rich backgrounds, always captivate me.

To create a limited edition is an art form in itself. They come from two sources: either the original animation or a conceptual drawing by a director or animator. At Warner Bros. it usually takes four to six months to bring a limited edition to life. One of the most difficult steps is knowing where to begin.

Much of our research is done watching cartoons and simply looking for inspiration. We also gather suggestions from collectors who are interested in a particular cartoon or character. Sometimes gallery

managers tell us what their clients would like to see as a limited-edition image. The final decision is made by balancing this feedback and devising a general business plan which keeps the characters and cartoon directors equally represented throughout a six-month period. Of course, we throw in our own ideas too.

Once an image is decided upon, we either work with archives to utilize the original animation or we "recreate the frame" by having a Polaroid print made off a television monitor. We then take the print and retrace the original animation. This step may sound easy, but it usually is not. A mediocre drawing can drain the life out of characters: Bugs might become just another rabbit and not the larger-than-life personality we have come to know. At WB I use what I consider to be the best young animation directors in the business, because it takes that kind of talent and finesse to do justice to the animation.

One advantage of the limited-edition medium is that we can make minor improvements: we can open a closed eye, or finish an arm cut off by a background, for example. This must be done cautiously so as to stay true to the original animation. We can fix missing whiskers or collars. We can even put two shots together to make one brilliant cel.

Once the drawing is finished, it is ready to be inked. Inking, the process of laying an acetate cel over a drawing and then outlining it in ink, is a highly skilled craft, although, due to the transition in animation to Xerox and computers, it is a dying art form. The quality of line on a cel is very important. A poorly inked cel hurts the image and can devalue an otherwise great drawing. At WBAA we create a *master inking* for our limited editions. A great inking will have transitions of very fine to medium lines, at times in a single stroke. The lines are clean and connected to preserve the integrity of the character design. A master inking can take hours to complete.

On most of our limited editions we then have the master ink lines silk-screened onto cels. This enables each cel in the edition to have the same flawless inking. Another advantage is that silk-screened lines are not as fragile as hand-inked. Hand-inked enhancements are often then done to create special effects such as movement (dry-brushing) or l.o.d.s (light on darks) to create separation when dark shapes overlap on a cel. Some studios use xerography for their line work, a process where the line is transferred by heat. Occasionally limited editions are created using hand-inking exclusively. This is a special feature that, when beautifully done, makes a limited edition unique.

After inking the characters' lines, a color model must be established for an edition. Here, every part of each character's color that will be filled in is matched to the original film. We have to be careful because many of the prints we view today are faded. I have had opportunities to view the original nitrate prints of many of my father's cartoons and was amazed by

TRAVIATA. Signed Limited Edition. Friz Freleng, 1992. With the director's uproarious *Back Alley Oproar* as its inspiration, *Traviata* depicts Sylvester at his most joyous, singing by moonlight. Alas, his gusto isn't shared by everyone.

LOONEY TUNES ON PARADE. Limited Edition.
Warner Bros. Classic Animation, 1993.

the vibrancy and richness of the original color. Oftentimes several color models are created before the final colors for an edition are established.

Cels are then assigned to painters who, while following the color model, meticulously paint the back of each cel. Colors are applied one at a time with some cels requiring dozens of colors. The hand painting is a special aspect of limited-edition cels. Good painting is difficult to achieve. There should be no overpaints (where the color overlaps onto the wrong side of the ink line) or streaky or thin paint (where the background bleeds through as dark spots on the paint color). I have always insisted on a higher standard for line quality and painting in limited editions because they are created to be framed and admired. There is no excuse for an imperfect cel.

A great background is also a key element to the success of a limited edition, for it is the marriage of cel and background that often tells the complete story of a scene. With limited editions from classic scenes, the original backgrounds are reproduced or recreated. With concept cels the background art is created to complement the scene.

At some point in the process of development the studio must make the difficult decision as to the number of images to create within an edition. Several factors must be considered. From one studio to the next I have seen the number produced vary from ten to twelve hundred. Often, the numbers reflect not only the strength of the image and its characters, but the philosophy of the publisher. The objective is to have enough cels to satisfy collectors but not so many that the edition doesn't sell out. Low edition sizes are very appealing, but they affect the final retail cost of a cel because they are so expensive to produce. As a publisher, I have experienced the wrath of collectors who did not have the opportunity to collect a favorite image because the edition size was too low. Once an

FORE! ... FIVE! ... Limited Edition. Warner Bros., 1996. Michael Jordan, whose "Hare Jordan" commercials for Nike launched a beautiful friendship with Bugs Bunny, went on to star with all the Looney Tunes characters in *Space Jam*. Here, all of them unwind on the links. Bogie?

image has been released at a given number it can never be changed or added to, no matter how popular the image.

The edition number will always be inked on the front of the cel. The certificate of authenticity that accompanies the cel should tell collectors the number of artist proofs that were created as part of the edition. Artist proofs are usually archived or kept by the artist, but they do affect the total number of cels created. Despite the debate over edition sizes, whether the final number of an edition is fifty or one thousand, I like to think that only a handful of collectors will ever own any one image.

Every studio has its philosophy for publishing limited editions. Some rely on concept or multiple character pieces, while others remain true to the original classic animation. With Warner Bros. Animation Art, we feature a variety of work from classics to concepts. Chuck Jones limited editions, for example, are created from his original drawings. He even inks his own master lines to insure that the final art is truly from his hand. This is rare in the world of animation, and certainly makes his art special. At WBAA we also have a reputation for creating unique art that incorporates everything from vintage art (such as model sheets and storyboards) to celebrities (such as Michael Jordan).

Warner Bros., The Disney Studio, and Hanna Barbera have always led the limited-edition market. Recently, however, many other studios have published limited editions of other characters. One would be hard pressed to think of a character that hasn't been featured in a limited edition, from Betty Boop to Speed Racer, Felix the Cat to The Simpsons. I have even seen limited editions of characters that never starred in a cartoon! As with any art market, the product can vary from the ridiculous to the sublime, with all measure of quality in between. But as long as there are enthusiastic collectors there will be a home for the full and varied family of animated characters.

Although limited editions were originally created to compensate for a lack of original production cels, today they are popular for other reasons as well. At WB, our Animation Department is currently producing "Batman: The Animated Series," and the original production cels from that show are very popular in our Studio Store Galleries. Last year we decided to release three limited editions inspired from "Batman" to test the market, and to our surprise, the limited editions are now sold out. Two more images released this year also sold out. This proves that by providing the optimum pose of characters with a great background, limited editions offer the collector an image that is a great alternative to a production cel.

How long will the limited-edition market last? Over the years I have heard doomsayers predict that the sensational growth of collecting this unique art form is short lived. Yet as each year passes, I've watched it grow. There was a period during which people were only interested in animation art as an investment due to the sensational prices that occurred

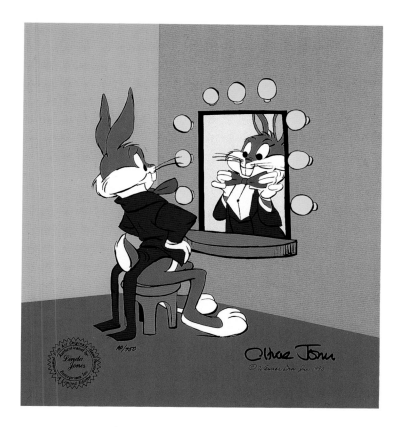

BUGS AND MIRROR. Signed Limited Edition. Chuck Jones, 1991.

at auction in the early 1990s. This type of investor will come and go, but the number of collectors who truly love the art and hang it in their homes and offices has grown steadily. When I got into the business no one outside the industry knew what a cel was. Now it's rare to find someone who is not aware of animation art. Animation galleries have expanded across the United States, Australia, and Europe, servicing collectors everywhere.

Animation is one of the most creative and expressive artistic mediums, and it is limited only by the boundaries of the imagination. We have all grown up with cartoons, so it is natural for us to want to preserve moments from those cartoons that have moved us or made us laugh. A framed animation cel is a treasured piece of history which draws us into its own unique world.

As a collector and art director, I often visit galleries to view the current animation art. What I look for first is a great image. Does it make you laugh or pull at your heart strings? Perhaps it is a classic image of your favorite character or simply a beautiful piece of art. My philosophy is that if you don't love it, don't buy it.

Next I examine the details of the art. The ink lines should be fine and unbroken, and the painting within these lines not thin or streaky. I then observe the background to see if it is reproduced by lithography, serigraph, photography, or color Xerox. The quality of the background reproduction and the paper it is printed on are also important aspects of the edition.

On the surface of the cel, I note the seal of authenticity from the publishing studio and the edition number, which has been inked by hand. The seal and certificate (usually attached to the back of the frame) verify its authenticity and provide valuable information about the edition.

Many limited editions will be hand signed by the directors who created or worked with the characters featured. This significantly adds value to a cel when the signature is from pioneers in the field of animation such as Friz Freleng, Chuck Jones, William Hanna, and Joseph Barbera. These cels certainly cost more than unsigned cels, but they are unique.

Because Bob Clampett Animation Art was instrumental in building the market for unsigned WB limited editions, I am often asked about the significance of a signature on a limited edition. When my family first got into the animation art business, many people discouraged us because we wouldn't be producing signed cels. But I always remembered that The Disney Studio's editions were not signed, and that they had some of the finest and most popular art on the market. Our efforts were also well received and our business grew, based on the knowledge that a signature (although certainly a wonderful addition) isn't always essential as long as you provide something special, of the highest quality. As I mentioned earlier, I always encourage people to collect because they love the image first and foremost, not because of its potential value, signed or unsigned.

When collecting animation art, I tell collectors to seek out reputable *and* authorized galleries, where they can build relationships with gallery directors or salespeople. I've found that the best gallery representatives are collectors themselves, who willingly share their knowledge and enthusiasm for the art form. Gallery managers can even network to help a collector find older or sold-out limited editions. They will also keep a client abreast of new releases and help locate special pieces. At our Warner Bros. Studio Stores, our gallery managers send out color cards of new images monthly to their collectors. Shopping at a reputable gallery also protects purchasers from obtaining forged or misrepresented art. The market for limited editions has stabilized and changed so that it is not a matter of shopping around for the lowest price anymore. A reputable gallery can offer you specialized services worthy of your patronage.

Once you bring your treasure home, treat it as you would any piece of fine art. Hang it securely, and away from extreme humidity or heat changes. Avoid hanging the art in bathrooms or near heating vents or radiators, and especially avoid any direct sunlight. Even a small amount of sun will cumulatively build up over time and cause fading. At Warner Bros., our art is framed archivally using acid-free mats. And always check the quality of your framing since that too can affect your art's long-term preservation.

One aspect in the development of the animation art market that has truly delighted me is the effect it has had on the classic cartoons and the people who worked on them. I often see people discovering or rediscovering cartoons through limited editions. In 1990, for example, my family published a suite of limited-edition cels from one of my father's

HIGH-DIVING SAM. Signed Limited Edition. Virgil Ross, 1994. Friz Freleng's masterly (and side-splitting) skills of comic timing and characterization clicked perfectly in *High-Diving Hare*, from which animator Virgil Ross's limited-edition cel is derived.

favorite cartoons, *Porky in Wackyland*. Until that point, this surreal 1938 black-and-white cartoon was known and revered by only the most knowledgeable animation fans.

Since our art release, I have watched the fan club for this cartoon grow steadily. Although the limited editions certainly are not solely responsible for *Wackyland*'s renaissance, I do believe they contributed to it.

Another example is talented Warner Bros. animator Virgil Ross, who rose out of obscurity due to his own collection of limited-edition cels. Never take for granted the impact a limited edition can have on the animation world.

In 1991, my family published The Model Series. This edition of four-character cels (Bugs, Daffy, Porky, and Tweety) were matched with reproductions of vintage model sheets. Now, a collector can go into a Warner Bros. Studio Store and see model sheets on everything from T-shirts to ties. As collectors learn more about the unique art and development of animation, their appreciation for drawings, model sheets, and storyboards grows.

People often ask me about my favorite limited edition. I have several, both from creators I have admired or characters I have loved. Most of all, though, I have to say that every Bob Clampett cel I have produced has come straight from the heart, each being a personal tribute to my father. He would be so pleased to know that collectors all over the world now own his images. I hope the same inspiration he shared with me I have shared with others. It continues to be an honor to play an important part in this industry, and I look forward to the years ahead.

AEROSPACE JORDAN (II): THAT'S ALL, FOLKS! Limited Edition. Created by Warner Bros. Classic Animation, 1994. The Warner Bros. Classic Animation division brought Bugs Bunny back to theater screens after a long absence, then launched him into a blockbuster relationship with superstar Michael Jordan. This cel is derived from the second commercial featuring both stars, two years before they appeared together in *Space Jam*.

Catalogue Raisonné of Warner Bros. Limited Edition Animation Art

1977

DUCK DODGERS GROUP
Chuck Jones
STYLE NO. CJ64000
EDITION SIZE: 500, CEL SIZE: 12F
ORIGINAL RETAIL PRICE: $135

1978

MOONLIGHTING
Chuck Jones
STYLE NO. CJ64001
EDITION SIZE: 50, CEL SIZE: 16F
ORIGINAL RETAIL PRICE: $175

1980

BUGS CLASSIC
Chuck Jones
STYLE NO. CJ00002
EDITION SIZE: 100, CEL SIZE: 12F
ORIGINAL RETAIL PRICE: $175

CLIFFHANGER
Chuck Jones
STYLE NO. CJ00003
EDITION SIZE: 100, CEL SIZE: 12F
ORIGINAL RETAIL PRICE: $175

HEARTTHROB PEPÉ
Chuck Jones
STYLE NO. CJ00004
EDITION SIZE: 50, CEL SIZE: 12F
ORIGINAL RETAIL PRICE: $175

MICHIGAN J. FROG
Chuck Jones
STYLE NO. CJ00001
EDITION SIZE: 50, CEL SIZE: 12F
ORIGINAL RETAIL PRICE: $175

WESTERN GROUP
Chuck Jones
STYLE NO. CJ65260
EDITION SIZE: 100, CEL SIZE: 16F
ORIGINAL RETAIL PRICE: $295

1981

ACME BATMAN
Chuck Jones
STYLE NO. CJ65341
EDITION SIZE: 100, CEL SIZE: 12F
ORIGINAL RETAIL PRICE: $175

BUGS AND BRIDE (I)
Chuck Jones
STYLE NO. CJ65345
EDITION SIZE: 200, CEL SIZE: 12F
ORIGINAL RETAIL PRICE: $250

DAFFY SHERLOCK (I)
Chuck Jones
STYLE NO. CJ65343
EDITION SIZE: 100, CEL SIZE: 12F
ORIGINAL RETAIL PRICE: $175

HEARTTHROB BUGS
Chuck Jones
STYLE NO. CJ00005
EDITION SIZE: 50, CEL SIZE: 12F
ORIGINAL RETAIL PRICE: $175

MISSED AGAIN
Chuck Jones
STYLE NO. CJ65351
EDITION SIZE: 100, CEL SIZE: 12F
ORIGINAL RETAIL PRICE: $175

MOUNTAIN CHASE
Chuck Jones
STYLE NO. CJ65353
EDITION SIZE: 200, CEL SIZE: 16F
ORIGINAL RETAIL PRICE: $195

TASMANIAN DEVIL (I)
Chuck Jones
STYLE NO. CJ65259
EDITION SIZE: 100, CEL SIZE: 12F
ORIGINAL RETAIL PRICE: $175

WHAT'S OPERA, DOC? (I)
Chuck Jones
STYLE NO. CJ65354
EDITION SIZE: 100, CEL SIZE: 12F
ORIGINAL RETAIL PRICE: $175

1982

GOLFING BUGS
Friz Freleng
STYLE NO. N/A
EDITION SIZE: 100, CEL SIZE: 12F
ORIGINAL RETAIL PRICE: $195

OUT ON A LIMB
Friz Freleng
STYLE NO. N/A
EDITION SIZE: 100, CEL SIZE: 12F
ORIGINAL RETAIL PRICE: $195

SPEEDY GONZALES
Friz Freleng
STYLE NO. N/A
EDITION SIZE: 100, CEL SIZE: 12F
ORIGINAL RETAIL PRICE: $195

TARGET PRACTICE
Friz Freleng
STYLE NO. N/A
EDITION SIZE: 100, CEL SIZE: 12F
ORIGINAL RETAIL PRICE: $195

TENNIS ANYONE?
Friz Freleng
STYLE NO. N/A
EDITION SIZE: 100, CEL SIZE: 12F
ORIGINAL RETAIL PRICE: $195

Tweety in the Rain
Friz Freleng
STYLE NO. N/A
EDITION SIZE: 100, CEL SIZE: 12F
ORIGINAL RETAIL PRICE: $195

Daffy Centerfold
Chuck Jones
STYLE NO. CJ34252
EDITION SIZE: 100, CEL SIZE: 12F
ORIGINAL RETAIL PRICE: $195

Two Gun Sam
Friz Freleng
STYLE NO. N/A
EDITION SIZE: 100, CEL SIZE: 12F
ORIGINAL RETAIL PRICE: $195

Dr. Bugs
Chuck Jones
STYLE NO. CJ34282
EDITION SIZE: 100, CEL SIZE: 12F
ORIGINAL RETAIL PRICE: $195

The Virtuoso
Friz Freleng
STYLE NO. N/A
EDITION SIZE: 100, CEL SIZE: 12F
ORIGINAL RETAIL PRICE: $195

Hunt and Found
Chuck Jones
STYLE NO. CJ34251
EDITION SIZE: 100, CEL SIZE: 12F
ORIGINAL RETAIL PRICE: $225

Bugs Centerfold
Chuck Jones
STYLE NO. CJ34242
EDITION SIZE: 100, CEL SIZE: 12F
ORIGINAL RETAIL PRICE: $195

Lunacy
Chuck Jones
STYLE NO. CJ34281
EDITION SIZE: 100, CEL SIZE: 12F
ORIGINAL RETAIL PRICE: $225

Cowboy Daffy
Chuck Jones
STYLE NO. CJ34286
EDITION SIZE: 100, CEL SIZE: 12F
ORIGINAL RETAIL PRICE: $195

Maitre D' Bugs
Chuck Jones
STYLE NO. CJ34285
EDITION SIZE: 100, CEL SIZE: 12F
ORIGINAL RETAIL PRICE: $195

NIGHT OF NIGHTS
Chuck Jones
STYLE NO. CJ34253
EDITION SIZE: 100, CEL SIZE: 12F
ORIGINAL RETAIL PRICE: $225

SANTA BUGS
Chuck Jones
STYLE NO. CJ34151
EDITION SIZE: 100, CEL SIZE: 12F
ORIGINAL RETAIL PRICE: $195

OLIVER WENDELL BUGS
Chuck Jones
STYLE NO. CJ36030
EDITION SIZE: 100, CEL SIZE: 12F
ORIGINAL RETAIL PRICE: $195

ROAD RUNNER CLASSIC
Chuck Jones
STYLE NO. CJ34283
EDITION SIZE: 200, CEL SIZE: 12F
ORIGINAL RETAIL PRICE: $195

PEPÉ IN FLOWERS
Chuck Jones
STYLE NO. CJ34241
EDITION SIZE: 100, CEL SIZE: 12F
ORIGINAL RETAIL PRICE: $195

SHERIFF BUGS
Chuck Jones
STYLE NO. CJ34284
EDITION SIZE: 100, CEL SIZE: 12F
ORIGINAL RETAIL PRICE: $195

PEPÉ L'AMOUR
Chuck Jones
STYLE NO. CJ34160
EDITION SIZE: 200, CEL SIZE: 12F
ORIGINAL RETAIL PRICE: $195

1983

TWAPPED
Friz Freleng
STYLE NO. N/A
EDITION SIZE: 100, CEL SIZE: 12F
ORIGINAL RETAIL PRICE: $225

ROAD RUNNER UNDER GLASS
Chuck Jones
STYLE NO. CJ34231
EDITION SIZE: 100, CEL SIZE: 16F
ORIGINAL RETAIL PRICE: $265

HOT PURSUIT
Chuck Jones
STYLE NO. CJ36085
EDITION SIZE: 200, CEL SIZE: 12F
ORIGINAL RETAIL PRICE: $295

HUNTING SEASON
Chuck Jones
STYLE NO. CJ36088
EDITION SIZE: 200, CEL SIZE: 12F
ORIGINAL RETAIL PRICE: $395

MAESTRO BUGS
Chuck Jones
STYLE NO. CJ36086
EDITION SIZE: 200, CEL SIZE: 12F
ORIGINAL RETAIL PRICE: $295

MICHIGAN J. FROG (II)
Chuck Jones
STYLE NO. CJ31351
EDITION SIZE: 200, CEL SIZE: 12F
ORIGINAL RETAIL PRICE: $225

PEPÉ LE ARCHER AND FIFI
Chuck Jones
STYLE NO. CJ36081
EDITION SIZE: 200, CEL SIZE: 12F
ORIGINAL RETAIL PRICE: $295

PEPÉ LE SATYR AND FIFI
Chuck Jones
STYLE NO. CJ36083
EDITION SIZE: 200, CEL SIZE: 12F
ORIGINAL RETAIL PRICE: $295

THE RACE IS ON!
Chuck Jones
STYLE NO. CJ36082
EDITION SIZE: 200, CEL SIZE: 12F
ORIGINAL RETAIL PRICE: $295

ROAD RUNNER IN FLIGHT
Chuck Jones
STYLE NO. CJ36084
EDITION SIZE: 200, CEL SIZE: 12F
ORIGINAL RETAIL PRICE: $295

SOMETHEENG?
Chuck Jones
STYLE NO. CJ36087
EDITION SIZE: 200, CEL SIZE: 12F
ORIGINAL RETAIL PRICE: $295

1984

PIRATE SAM
Friz Freleng
STYLE NO. N/A
EDITION SIZE: 200, CEL SIZE: 12F
ORIGINAL RETAIL PRICE: $225

WHIRLING DERVISH
Friz Freleng
STYLE NO. N/A
EDITION SIZE: 200, CEL SIZE: 12F
ORIGINAL RETAIL PRICE: $225

DAFFY SHERLOCK (II)
Chuck Jones
STYLE NO. CJ73831
EDITION SIZE: 200, CEL SIZE: 12F
ORIGINAL RETAIL PRICE: $295

PORKY WATSON
Chuck Jones
STYLE NO. CJ73922
EDITION SIZE: 200, CEL SIZE: 12F
ORIGINAL RETAIL PRICE: $295

FOGHORN AND HENERY
Chuck Jones
STYLE NO. CJ73811
EDITION SIZE: 200, CEL SIZE: 12F
ORIGINAL RETAIL PRICE: $225

1985

BUGS HEAD
Bob Clampett
STYLE NO. N/A
EDITION SIZE: 250, CEL SIZE: 12F
ORIGINAL RETAIL PRICE: $225

THE GREAT CHASE
Chuck Jones
STYLE NO. CJ73721
EDITION SIZE: 200, CEL SIZE: 16F
ORIGINAL RETAIL PRICE: $295

CLASSIC BUGS
Bob Clampett
STYLE NO. N/A
EDITION SIZE: 250, CEL SIZE: 12F
ORIGINAL RETAIL PRICE: $225

MARVIN MARTIAN AND BUGS
Chuck Jones
STYLE NO. CJ73860
EDITION SIZE: 200, CEL SIZE: 12F
ORIGINAL RETAIL PRICE: $295

CLASSIC PORKY
Bob Clampett
STYLE NO. N/A
EDITION SIZE: 250, CEL SIZE: 12F
ORIGINAL RETAIL PRICE: $225

NIGHT OF NIGHTS (II)
Chuck Jones
STYLE NO. CJ73612
EDITION SIZE: 200, CEL SIZE: 12F
ORIGINAL RETAIL PRICE: $295

PALM SPRINGS GROUP
Chuck Jones
STYLE NO. CJ73722
EDITION SIZE: 200, CEL SIZE: 16F
ORIGINAL RETAIL PRICE: $295

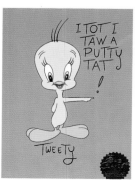

CLASSIC TWEETY
Bob Clampett
STYLE NO. N/A
EDITION SIZE: 250, CEL SIZE: 12F
ORIGINAL RETAIL PRICE: $225

DAFFY HEAD
Bob Clampett
STYLE NO. N/A
EDITION SIZE: 250, CEL SIZE: 12F
ORIGINAL RETAIL PRICE: $225

TWEETY HEAD
Bob Clampett
STYLE NO. N/A
EDITION SIZE: 250, CEL SIZE: 12F
ORIGINAL RETAIL PRICE: $225

BULLY FOR BUGS
Chuck Jones
STYLE NO. CJ36302
EDITION SIZE: 200, CEL SIZE: 12F
ORIGINAL RETAIL PRICE: $295

ENCORE
Chuck Jones
STYLE NO. CJ40052
EDITION SIZE: 200, CEL SIZE: 12F
ORIGINAL RETAIL PRICE: $295

PHONEY BUNNY
Chuck Jones
STYLE NO. CJ73925
EDITION SIZE: 200, CEL SIZE: 12F
ORIGINAL RETAIL PRICE: $295

SCARLET PUMPERNICKLE
Chuck Jones
STYLE NO. CJ40023
EDITION SIZE: 200, CEL SIZE: 12F
ORIGINAL RETAIL PRICE: $295

SHERWOOD FOREST
Chuck Jones
STYLE NO. CJ40012
EDITION SIZE: 200, CEL SIZE: 12F
ORIGINAL RETAIL PRICE: $295

WHAT'S OPERA, DOC? (II)
Chuck Jones
STYLE NO. CJ36301
EDITION SIZE: 200, CEL SIZE: 16F
ORIGINAL RETAIL PRICE: $395

1986

AHH HATES VARMINTS
Friz Freleng
STYLE NO. N/A
EDITION SIZE: 200, CEL SIZE: 12F
ORIGINAL RETAIL PRICE: $295

CHAMPION MOUSER
Friz Freleng
STYLE NO. FF1026
EDITION SIZE: 200, CEL SIZE: 12F
ORIGINAL RETAIL PRICE: $295

DUCK HUNTING
Friz Freleng
STYLE NO. N/A
EDITION SIZE: 100, CEL SIZE: 12F
ORIGINAL RETAIL PRICE: $295

HIGH DIVING HARE (I)
Friz Freleng
STYLE NO. N/A
EDITION SIZE: 100, CEL SIZE: 12F
ORIGINAL RETAIL PRICE: $295

PEEPING TOM (I)
Friz Freleng
STYLE NO. N/A
EDITION SIZE: 100, CEL SIZE: 12F
ORIGINAL RETAIL PRICE: $295

SHOWDOWN (I)
Friz Freleng
STYLE NO. N/A
EDITION SIZE: 100, CEL SIZE: 12F
ORIGINAL RETAIL PRICE: $295

ACME SNOW MACHINE
Chuck Jones
STYLE NO. CJ80114
EDITION SIZE: 200, CEL SIZE: 12F
ORIGINAL RETAIL PRICE: $295

BIRTHDAY BUGS
Chuck Jones
STYLE NO. CJ40042
EDITION SIZE: 200, CEL SIZE: 12F
ORIGINAL RETAIL PRICE: $295

BUGS AND BRIDE (II)
Chuck Jones
STYLE NO. CJ40032
EDITION SIZE: 200, CEL SIZE: 12F
ORIGINAL RETAIL PRICE: $295

DAFFY DADDY
Chuck Jones
STYLE NO. CJ80102
EDITION SIZE: 200, CEL SIZE: 12F
ORIGINAL RETAIL PRICE: $295

DAFFY DUCK AND DR. HI
Chuck Jones
STYLE NO. CJ80082
EDITION SIZE: 200, CEL SIZE: 12F
ORIGINAL RETAIL PRICE: $295

DAFFY SANTA
Chuck Jones
STYLE NO. CJ80141
EDITION SIZE: 200, CEL SIZE: 12F
ORIGINAL RETAIL PRICE: $295

DEVIL'S FOOD
Chuck Jones
STYLE NO. CJ80061
EDITION SIZE: 200, CEL SIZE: 12F
ORIGINAL RETAIL PRICE: $295

HIGH STRUNG COYOTE
Chuck Jones
STYLE NO. CJ80122
EDITION SIZE: 200, CEL SIZE: 12F
ORIGINAL RETAIL PRICE: $295

KISS AND MAKE UP
Friz Freleng
STYLE NO. N/A
EDITION SIZE: 200, CEL SIZE: 12F
ORIGINAL RETAIL PRICE: $350

MARK ANTHONY AND KITTY
Chuck Jones
STYLE NO. CJ80072
EDITION SIZE: 200, CEL SIZE: 12F
ORIGINAL RETAIL PRICE: $295

SHOW STOPPER
Friz Freleng
STYLE NO. N/A
EDITION SIZE: 200, CEL SIZE: 12F
ORIGINAL RETAIL PRICE: $350

RABBIT SEASONING
Chuck Jones
STYLE NO. CJ80093
EDITION SIZE: 200, CEL SIZE: 12F
ORIGINAL RETAIL PRICE: $295

TAKE 14
Friz Freleng
STYLE NO. N/A
EDITION SIZE: 200, CEL SIZE: 12F
ORIGINAL RETAIL PRICE: $350

SANTA BUGS WITH BUNNY
Chuck Jones
STYLE NO. CJ80132
EDITION SIZE: 200, CEL SIZE: 12F
ORIGINAL RETAIL PRICE: $295

TWEETY'S SERENADE
Friz Freleng
STYLE NO. N/A
EDITION SIZE: 200, CEL SIZE: 12F
ORIGINAL RETAIL PRICE: $350

1987

BAD PUDDY TAT
Friz Freleng
STYLE NO. FF1044
EDITION SIZE: 500, CEL SIZE: 12F
ORIGINAL RETAIL PRICE: $350

WHAZZAT, SON?
Friz Freleng
STYLE NO. FF1031
EDITION SIZE: 200, CEL SIZE: 12F
ORIGINAL RETAIL PRICE: $350

JUNE BRIDE
Friz Freleng
STYLE NO. N/A
EDITION SIZE: 200, CEL SIZE: 12F
ORIGINAL RETAIL PRICE: $350

BUGS AND DAFFY: EXIT STAGE LEFT
Chuck Jones
STYLE NO. CJ80152
EDITION SIZE: 200, CEL SIZE: 12F
ORIGINAL RETAIL PRICE: $295

BUGS AND WITCH HAZEL (I)
Chuck Jones
STYLE NO. CJ80282
EDITION SIZE: 200, CEL SIZE: 12F
ORIGINAL RETAIL PRICE: $295

HELLO RALPH, HELLO SAM
Chuck Jones
STYLE NO. CJ80302
EDITION SIZE: 200, CEL SIZE: 12F
ORIGINAL RETAIL PRICE: $295

BUNNYBACK RIDE
Chuck Jones
STYLE NO. CJ80312
EDITION SIZE: 200, CEL SIZE: 12F
ORIGINAL RETAIL PRICE: $295

LAST CHANCE SALOON
Chuck Jones
STYLE NO. CJ80279
EDITION SIZE: 500, CEL SIZE: 16F
ORIGINAL RETAIL PRICE: $495

CONTEMPT IN COURT
Chuck Jones
STYLE NO. CJ80232
EDITION SIZE: 200, CEL SIZE: 12F
ORIGINAL RETAIL PRICE: $295

MICHIGAN RAG
Chuck Jones
STYLE NO. CJ80221
EDITION SIZE: 200, CEL SIZE: 12F
ORIGINAL RETAIL PRICE: $295

DENTIST BUGS
Chuck Jones
STYLE NO. CJ80192
EDITION SIZE: 200, CEL SIZE: 12F
ORIGINAL RETAIL PRICE: $295

DUCK DODGERS (II)
Chuck Jones
STYLE NO. CJ80262
EDITION SIZE: 200, CEL SIZE: 12F
ORIGINAL RETAIL PRICE: $295

OPEN SEASON
Chuck Jones
STYLE NO. CJ80292
EDITION SIZE: 200, CEL SIZE: 12F
ORIGINAL RETAIL PRICE: $295

RABBIT OF SEVILLE (I)
Chuck Jones
STYLE NO. CJ80162
EDITION SIZE: 200, CEL SIZE: 12F
ORIGINAL RETAIL PRICE: $295

HASSAN CHOP
Chuck Jones
STYLE NO. CJ80252
EDITION SIZE: 200, CEL SIZE: 12F
ORIGINAL RETAIL PRICE: $295

ROAD RUNNER RECIPES
Chuck Jones
STYLE NO. CJ80182
EDITION SIZE: 200, CEL SIZE: 12F
ORIGINAL RETAIL PRICE: $295

HIGH DIVING HARE (II)
Friz Freleng
STYLE NO. N/A
EDITION SIZE: 300, CEL SIZE: 16F
ORIGINAL RETAIL PRICE: $350

SURFIN' BUGS
Chuck Jones
STYLE NO. CJ80201
EDITION SIZE: 200, CEL SIZE: 12F
ORIGINAL RETAIL PRICE: $295

PEEPING TOM (II)
Friz Freleng
STYLE NO. N/A
EDITION SIZE: 500, CEL SIZE: 12F
ORIGINAL RETAIL PRICE: $395

1988

BUGS COURTS BONNIE
Friz Freleng
STYLE NO. FF1030
EDITION SIZE: 300, CEL SIZE: 12F
ORIGINAL RETAIL PRICE: $350

THE SHOWDOWN (II)
Friz Freleng
STYLE NO. N/A
EDITION SIZE: 300, CEL SIZE: 12F
ORIGINAL RETAIL PRICE: $350

CIRCUS
Friz Freleng
STYLE NO. N/A
EDITION SIZE: 500, CEL SIZE: 16F
ORIGINAL RETAIL PRICE: $495

SYLVESTER AND SON (I)
Friz Freleng
STYLE NO. FF1022
EDITION SIZE: 300, CEL SIZE: 12F
ORIGINAL RETAIL PRICE: $350

TAZ AND BRIDE (I)
Friz Freleng
STYLE NO. FF1029
EDITION SIZE: 200, CEL SIZE: 12F
ORIGINAL RETAIL PRICE: $350

FINALE
Friz Freleng
STYLE NO. N/A
EDITION SIZE: 750, CEL SIZE: 12F (pan)
ORIGINAL RETAIL PRICE: $695

BIRTHDAY CARD
Chuck Jones
STYLE NO. CJ80442
EDITION SIZE: 500, CEL SIZE: 12F
ORIGINAL RETAIL PRICE: $350

BULLY FOR BUGS (II)
Chuck Jones
STYLE NO. CJ80502
EDITION SIZE: 500, CEL SIZE: 16F
ORIGINAL RETAIL PRICE: $595

THE CATS BAH
Chuck Jones
STYLE NO. CJ80342
EDITION SIZE: 300, CEL SIZE: 12F
ORIGINAL RETAIL PRICE: $295

BIRTH OF A NOTION
Chuck Jones
STYLE NO. CJ80374
EDITION SIZE: 500, CEL SIZE: 16F (pan)
ORIGINAL RETAIL PRICE: $695

DAFFY TENNIS
Chuck Jones
STYLE NO. CJ80321
EDITION SIZE: 300, CEL SIZE: 12F
ORIGINAL RETAIL PRICE: $295

BUGS AND DAFFY: APPLAUSE
Chuck Jones
STYLE NO. CJ80412
EDITION SIZE: 500, CEL SIZE: 12F
ORIGINAL RETAIL PRICE: $565

DR. DAFFY AND BUGS
Chuck Jones
STYLE NO. CJ80452
EDITION SIZE: 500, CEL SIZE: 12F
ORIGINAL RETAIL PRICE: $350

BUGS AND MARVIN MARTIAN
Chuck Jones
STYLE NO. CJ80392
EDITION SIZE: 300, CEL SIZE: 12F
ORIGINAL RETAIL PRICE: $350

DRIP-ALONG DAFFY
Chuck Jones
STYLE NO. CJ80401
EDITION SIZE: 300, CEL SIZE: 12F
ORIGINAL RETAIL PRICE: $350

BUGS TENNIS
Chuck Jones
STYLE NO. CJ80381
EDITION SIZE: 300, CEL SIZE: 12F
ORIGINAL RETAIL PRICE: $350

HENERY HAWK STRIKES AGAIN
Chuck Jones
STYLE NO. CJ80362
EDITION SIZE: 300, CEL SIZE: 12F
ORIGINAL RETAIL PRICE: $295

SHAKE HANDS WITH FRIAR DUCK
Chuck Jones
STYLE NO. CJ80472
EDITION SIZE: 500, CEL SIZE: 12F
ORIGINAL RETAIL PRICE: $350

HOT PURSUIT (II)
Chuck Jones
STYLE NO. CJ80432
EDITION SIZE: 300, CEL SIZE: 16F
ORIGINAL RETAIL PRICE: $495

SHOW TIME
Chuck Jones
STYLE NO. CJ80172
EDITION SIZE: 500, CEL SIZE: 12F
ORIGINAL RETAIL PRICE: $295

MARRIAGE MADE IN HEAVEN
Chuck Jones
STYLE NO. CJ80423
EDITION SIZE: 500, CEL SIZE: 12F
ORIGINAL RETAIL PRICE: $350

WHAT'S THE VERDICT?
Chuck Jones
STYLE NO. CJ80353
EDITION SIZE: 300, CEL SIZE: 12F
ORIGINAL RETAIL PRICE: $295

PRONOUN TROUBLE
Chuck Jones
STYLE NO. CJ80332
EDITION SIZE: 300, CEL SIZE: 12F
ORIGINAL RETAIL PRICE: $295

1989

BABY BOTTLENECK
Bob Clampett
STYLE NO. BC1003
EDITION SIZE: 500, CEL SIZE: 12F
ORIGINAL RETAIL PRICE: $425

THE RABBIT OF SEVILLE (II)
Chuck Jones
STYLE NO. CJ80462
EDITION SIZE: 500, CEL SIZE: 12F
ORIGINAL RETAIL PRICE: $425

BUGS BUNNY GETS THE BOID
Bob Clampett
STYLE NO. BC1004
EDITION SIZE: 500, CEL SIZE: 12F
ORIGINAL RETAIL PRICE: $425

GREAT PIGGY BANK ROBBERY
Bob Clampett
STYLE NO. BC1002
EDITION SIZE: 500, CEL SIZE: 12F
ORIGINAL RETAIL PRICE: $425

BIRDY AND THE BEAST
Bob Clampett
STYLE NO. BC1001
EDITION SIZE: 500, CEL SIZE: 12F
ORIGINAL RETAIL PRICE: $425

CLAWS FOR ALARM
Chuck Jones
STYLE NO. CJ80562
EDITION SIZE: 500, CEL SIZE: 12F
ORIGINAL RETAIL PRICE: $275

KNIGHTY KNIGHT BUGS
Friz Freleng
STYLE NO. N/A
EDITION SIZE: 500, CEL SIZE: 12F
ORIGINAL RETAIL PRICE: $395

DAFFY CAVALIER
Chuck Jones
STYLE NO. CJ80511
EDITION SIZE: 500, CEL SIZE: 12F
ORIGINAL RETAIL PRICE: $350

TAZ AND BRIDE (II)
Friz Freleng
STYLE NO. N/A
EDITION SIZE: 750, CEL SIZE: 12F
ORIGINAL RETAIL PRICE: $525

DAFFY'S IMPOSSIBLE DREAM
Chuck Jones
STYLE NO. CJ80532
EDITION SIZE: 500, CEL SIZE: 12F
ORIGINAL RETAIL PRICE: $350

THAT'S ALL, FOLKS!
Friz Freleng
STYLE NO. N/A
EDITION SIZE: 500, CEL SIZE: 16F
ORIGINAL RETAIL PRICE: $475

DAFFY SHERLOCK AND YOSEMITE
Chuck Jones
STYLE NO. CJ80582
EDITION SIZE: 500, CEL SIZE: 12F
ORIGINAL RETAIL PRICE: $475

WHAT'S UP, DOC?
Friz Freleng
STYLE NO. N/A
EDITION SIZE: 750, CEL SIZE: 12F
ORIGINAL RETAIL PRICE: $495

DIRECTOR BUGS
Chuck Jones
STYLE NO. CJ80602
EDITION SIZE: 500, CEL SIZE: 16F
ORIGINAL RETAIL PRICE: $1,110

BABY CHASE
Chuck Jones
STYLE NO. CJ80482
EDITION SIZE: 500, CEL SIZE: 12F
ORIGINAL RETAIL PRICE: $350

DR. BUGS (II)
Chuck Jones
STYLE NO. CJ80611
EDITION SIZE: 500, CEL SIZE: 12F
ORIGINAL RETAIL PRICE: $520

WHAT'S OPERA, DOC? (III)
Chuck Jones
STYLE NO. CJ80492
EDITION SIZE: 500, CEL SIZE: 16F
ORIGINAL RETAIL PRICE: $595

HAIR-RAISING HARE
Chuck Jones
STYLE NO. CJ80552
EDITION SIZE: 500, CEL SIZE: 12F
ORIGINAL RETAIL PRICE: $425

BUGS ON STAGE
Robert McKimson
STYLE NO. BM50011
EDITION SIZE: 500, CEL SIZE: 12F
ORIGINAL RETAIL PRICE: $450

PEPÉ IN TULIPS
Chuck Jones
STYLE NO. CJ80521
EDITION SIZE: 500, CEL SIZE: 12F
ORIGINAL RETAIL PRICE: $350

DAFFY DUCK
Robert McKimson
STYLE NO. BM50031
EDITION SIZE: 500, CEL SIZE: 12F
ORIGINAL RETAIL PRICE: $450

ROAD RUNNER CLASSIC (II)
Chuck Jones
STYLE NO. CJ80541
EDITION SIZE: 500, CEL SIZE: 12F
ORIGINAL RETAIL PRICE: $350

TASMANIAN DEVIL
Robert McKimson
STYLE NO. BM50021
EDITION SIZE: 500, CEL SIZE: 12F
ORIGINAL RETAIL PRICE: $450

TRADERS
Chuck Jones
STYLE NO. CJ80592
EDITION SIZE: 500, CEL SIZE: 12F
ORIGINAL RETAIL PRICE: $495

1990

ANY BONDS TODAY?
Bob Clampett
STYLE NO. BC1008
EDITION SIZE: 500, CEL SIZE: 12F
ORIGINAL RETAIL PRICE: $450

BUGS AND BEAKY JITTERBUG
Bob Clampett
STYLE NO. BC1005
EDITION SIZE: 500, CEL SIZE: 12F
ORIGINAL RETAIL PRICE: $425

CHORUS LINE
Friz Freleng
STYLE NO. FF1002
EDITION SIZE: 1,200, CEL SIZE: 16F
ORIGINAL RETAIL PRICE: $1,225

WHAT'S COOKIN', DOC?
Bob Clampett
STYLE NO. BC1007
EDITION SIZE: 500, CEL SIZE: 12F
ORIGINAL RETAIL PRICE: $450

HAPPY BIRTHDAY BUGS!
Friz Freleng
STYLE NO. FF1004
EDITION SIZE: 750, CEL SIZE: 12F
ORIGINAL RETAIL PRICE: $695

DAFFY FINDS HIS PIGGYBANK
Bob Clampett
STYLE NO. BC1006
EDITION SIZE: 500, CEL SIZE: 12F
ORIGINAL RETAIL PRICE: $425

WHO DONE IT?
Friz Freleng
STYLE NO. FF1039
EDITION SIZE: 750, CEL SIZE: 16F
ORIGINAL RETAIL PRICE: $595

BASEBALL BUGS
Friz Freleng
STYLE NO. FF1038
EDITION SIZE: 1,200, CEL SIZE: 16F
ORIGINAL RETAIL PRICE: $795

BUGS AND MIRROR
Chuck Jones
STYLE NO. CJ80671
EDITION SIZE: 750, CEL SIZE: 12F
ORIGINAL RETAIL PRICE: $475

BUGS THE STAR
Friz Freleng
STYLE NO. FF1003
EDITION SIZE: 750, CEL SIZE: 16F
ORIGINAL RETAIL PRICE: $595

CALL ME A CAB
Chuck Jones
STYLE NO. CJ80652
EDITION SIZE: 500, CEL SIZE: 16F
ORIGINAL RETAIL PRICE: $700

THE CELEBRATION
Friz Freleng
STYLE NO. FF1005
EDITION SIZE: 750, CEL SIZE: 16F
ORIGINAL RETAIL PRICE: $695

DUCK DODGERS TRIO
Chuck Jones
STYLE NO. CJ80693
EDITION SIZE: 750, CEL SIZE: 12F
ORIGINAL RETAIL PRICE: $775

DUCKLARATION
Chuck Jones
STYLE NO. CJ80665
EDITION SIZE: 500, CEL SIZE: 16F
ORIGINAL RETAIL PRICE: $765

QUINTET
Chuck Jones
STYLE NO. CJ80626
EDITION SIZE: 500, CEL SIZE: 16F (pan)
ORIGINAL RETAIL PRICE: $1,110

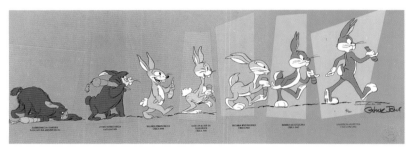

EVOLUTION OF BUGS
Chuck Jones
STYLE NO. CJ80707
EDITION SIZE: 750, CEL SIZE: 16F (pan)
ORIGINAL RETAIL PRICE: $1,260

SKIING
Chuck Jones
STYLE NO. CJ80642
EDITION SIZE: 500, CEL SIZE: 12F
ORIGINAL RETAIL PRICE: $520

MICHIGAN J. FROG (IV)
Chuck Jones
STYLE NO. CJ80631
EDITION SIZE: 500, CEL SIZE: 12F
ORIGINAL RETAIL PRICE: $475

FOGHORN LEGHORN
Robert McKimson
STYLE NO. BM50041
EDITION SIZE: 750, CEL SIZE: 12F
ORIGINAL RETAIL PRICE: $450

BUGS WITH CARROT
Robert McKimson
STYLE NO. BM50051
EDITION SIZE: 750, CEL SIZE: 12F
ORIGINAL RETAIL PRICE: $450

A WILD HARE
Warner Bros. Classic Animation
  Bugs Bunny 50th Anniversary
  Collector's Edition
STYLE NO. N/A
EDITION SIZE: 500, CEL SIZE: 12F
ORIGINAL RETAIL PRICE: $500

THE OLD GREY HARE
Warner Bros. Classic Animation
  Bugs Bunny 50th Anniversary
  Collector's Edition
STYLE NO. N/A
EDITION SIZE: 500, CEL SIZE: 12F
ORIGINAL RETAIL PRICE: $500

BIG HOUSE BUNNY
Warner Bros. Classic Animation
  Bugs Bunny 50th Anniversary
  Collector's Edition
STYLE NO. N/A
EDITION SIZE: 500, CEL SIZE: 12F
ORIGINAL RETAIL PRICE: $500

RABBIT FIRE
Warner Bros. Classic Animation
  Bugs Bunny 50th Anniversary
  Collector's Edition
STYLE NO. N/A
EDITION SIZE: 500, CEL SIZE: 12F
ORIGINAL RETAIL PRICE: $500

A-LAD-IN HIS LAMP
Warner Bros. Classic Animation
  Bugs Bunny 50th Anniversary
  Collector's Edition
STYLE NO. N/A
EDITION SIZE: 500, CEL SIZE: 12F
ORIGINAL RETAIL PRICE: $500

1991

BUGS MODEL SHEET
Bob Clampett
STYLE NO. N/A
EDITION SIZE: 500, CEL SIZE: 16F
ORIGINAL RETAIL PRICE: $450

DAFFY MODEL SHEET
Bob Clampett
STYLE NO. N/A
EDITION SIZE: 500, CEL SIZE: 16F
ORIGINAL RETAIL PRICE: $450

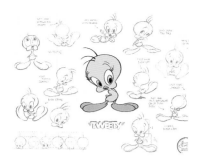

TWEETY MODEL SHEET
Bob Clampett
STYLE NO. N/A
EDITION SIZE: 500, CEL SIZE: 16F
ORIGINAL RETAIL PRICE: $450

WELCOME TO WACKYLAND
Bob Clampett
STYLE NO. BC1006
EDITION SIZE: 500, CEL SIZE: 12F
ORIGINAL RETAIL PRICE: $430

INFORMATION ABOUT THE DO-DO
Bob Clampett
STYLE NO. BC1007
EDITION SIZE: 500, CEL SIZE: 12F
ORIGINAL RETAIL PRICE: $430

SLINGSHOT SHIELD
Bob Clampett
STYLE NO. BC1008
EDITION SIZE: 500, CEL SIZE: 12F
ORIGINAL RETAIL PRICE: $430

WOO-WOO!
Bob Clampett
STYLE NO. BC1009
EDITION SIZE: 500, CEL SIZE: 12F
ORIGINAL RETAIL PRICE: $430

LAST OF THE DO-DOS
Bob Clampett
STYLE NO. BC1010
EDITION SIZE: 500, CEL SIZE: 12F
ORIGINAL RETAIL PRICE: $430

PUDDLE BEACH
Friz Freleng
STYLE NO. FF1028
EDITION SIZE: 500, CEL SIZE: 16F
ORIGINAL RETAIL PRICE: $975

PORKY MODEL SHEET
Bob Clampett
STYLE NO. N/A
EDITION SIZE: 500, CEL SIZE: 16F
ORIGINAL RETAIL PRICE: $450

RHAPSODY RABBIT
Friz Freleng
STYLE NO. FF1032
EDITION SIZE: 750, CEL SIZE: 12F
ORIGINAL RETAIL PRICE: $525

THE ACROBATS
Friz Freleng
STYLE NO. FF1007
EDITION SIZE: 750, CEL SIZE: 16F (pan)
ORIGINAL RETAIL PRICE: $1,175

THE SQUIRT
Friz Freleng
STYLE NO. FF1037
EDITION SIZE: 500, CEL SIZE: 12F
ORIGINAL RETAIL PRICE: $675

BIRDS OF A FEATHER
Friz Freleng
STYLE NO. FF1009
EDITION SIZE: 500, CEL SIZE: 12F
ORIGINAL RETAIL PRICE: $600

SYLVESTER AND SON (II)
Friz Freleng
STYLE NO. FF1001
EDITION SIZE: 500, CEL SIZE: 16F (pan)
ORIGINAL RETAIL PRICE: $595

THE ENTERTAINERS
Friz Freleng
STYLE NO. FF1006
EDITION SIZE: 1,200, CEL SIZE: 16F
ORIGINAL RETAIL PRICE: $825

ACME BATMAN
Chuck Jones
STYLE NO. CJ80821
EDITION SIZE: 100, CEL SIZE: 12F
ORIGINAL RETAIL PRICE: $525

NO SMOKING
Friz Freleng
STYLE NO. FF1008
EDITION SIZE: 750, CEL SIZE: 16F
ORIGINAL RETAIL PRICE: $595

BUGS: AUTOMATIC BATTER
Chuck Jones
STYLE NO. CJ80881
EDITION SIZE: 100, CEL SIZE: 12F
ORIGINAL RETAIL PRICE: $600

THE FANATIC
Chuck Jones
STYLE NO. CJ80712
EDITION SIZE: 750, CEL SIZE: 16F (pan)
ORIGINAL RETAIL PRICE: $1,225

CLOUD 9
Chuck Jones
STYLE NO. CJ80682
EDITION SIZE: 750, CEL SIZE: 12F
ORIGINAL RETAIL PRICE: $575

GRAVITY: ROAD RUNNER
  AND WILE E. COYOTE
Chuck Jones
STYLE NO. CJ80812
EDITION SIZE: 100, CEL SIZE: 12F
ORIGINAL RETAIL PRICE: $750

DANCES WITH WABBITS
Chuck Jones
STYLE NO. CJ80762
EDITION SIZE: 500, CEL SIZE: 16F
ORIGINAL RETAIL PRICE: $750

HAPPY NEW YEAR
Chuck Jones
STYLE NO. CJ80731
EDITION SIZE: 100, CEL SIZE: 12F
ORIGINAL RETAIL PRICE: $525

COURTROOM
Chuck Jones
STYLE NO. CJ80902
EDITION SIZE: 500, CEL SIZE: 12F
ORIGINAL RETAIL PRICE: $550

DUCK SEASON, WABBIT SEASON
Chuck Jones
STYLE NO. CJ80852
EDITION SIZE: 100, CEL SIZE: 12F
ORIGINAL RETAIL PRICE: $600

HAREWAY TO THE STARS
Chuck Jones
STYLE NO. CJ80772
EDITION SIZE: 187, CEL SIZE: 12F
ORIGINAL RETAIL PRICE: $750

EVENIN' SAM, EVENIN' RALPH
Chuck Jones
STYLE NO. CJ80872
EDITION SIZE: 100, CEL SIZE: 12F
ORIGINAL RETAIL PRICE: $600

HOLD THE MUSTARD
Chuck Jones
STYLE NO. CJ80841
EDITION SIZE: 100, CEL SIZE: 12F
ORIGINAL RETAIL PRICE: $600

MARK ANTHONY AND KITTY (II)
Chuck Jones
STYLE NO. CJ80742
EDITION SIZE: 750, CEL SIZE: 12F
ORIGINAL RETAIL PRICE: $575

VALENTINE BUGS
Chuck Jones
STYLE NO. CJ80922
EDITION SIZE: 500, CEL SIZE: 12F
ORIGINAL RETAIL PRICE: $550

N.T.L. CHANCE SALOON
Chuck Jones
STYLE NO. CJ80727
EDITION SIZE: 750, CEL SIZE: 16F
ORIGINAL RETAIL PRICE: $835

WILE E. COYOTE—PITCHER
Chuck Jones
STYLE NO. CJ80891
EDITION SIZE: 100, CEL SIZE: 12F
ORIGINAL RETAIL PRICE: $600

PEPÉ LE PEW AT BAT
Chuck Jones
STYLE NO. CJ80861
EDITION SIZE: 100, CEL SIZE: 12F
ORIGINAL RETAIL PRICE: $600

COYOTE STRIKES AGAIN
Robert McKimson
STYLE NO. BM2005
EDITION SIZE: 500, CEL SIZE: 12F
ORIGINAL RETAIL PRICE: $550

PEPÉ LE SNIFF
Chuck Jones
STYLE NO. CJ80791
EDITION SIZE: 100, CEL SIZE: 12F
ORIGINAL RETAIL PRICE: $525

HIPPETY'S MUMMY
Robert McKimson
STYLE NO. BM2000
EDITION SIZE: 500, CEL SIZE: 12F
ORIGINAL RETAIL PRICE: $550

HOLLYWOOD HARE
Robert McKimson
STYLE NO. BM2003
EDITION SIZE: 500, CEL SIZE: 12F
ORIGINAL RETAIL PRICE: $550

SOUNDSTAGE
Chuck Jones
STYLE NO. CJ80756
EDITION SIZE: 750, CEL SIZE: 16F (pan)
ORIGINAL RETAIL PRICE: $1,425

LET'S PLAY CROQUET
Robert McKimson
STYLE NO. BM2004
EDITION SIZE: 500, CEL SIZE: 12F
ORIGINAL RETAIL PRICE: $500

LOOK, NO MEAT!
Robert McKimson
STYLE NO. BM1000
EDITION SIZE: 500, CEL SIZE: 12F
ORIGINAL RETAIL PRICE: $550

DR. BUGS AND TAZ
Warner Bros. Sericels
STYLE NO. N/A
EDITION SIZE: 250, CEL SIZE: 12F
ORIGINAL RETAIL PRICE: $175

VINTAGE BUGS
Robert McKimson
STYLE NO. BM2500
EDITION SIZE: 750, CEL SIZE: 16F
ORIGINAL RETAIL PRICE: $475

Image Not Available

FOGHORN AND HENERY HAWK
Warner Bros. Sericels
STYLE NO. N/A
EDITION SIZE: 250, CEL SIZE: 12F
ORIGINAL RETAIL PRICE: $175

HARE TRIMMED
Warner Bros./Freleng
STYLE NO. N/A
EDITION SIZE: 100, CEL SIZE: 12F
ORIGINAL RETAIL PRICE: $725

RABBIT FIRE
Warner Bros. Sericels
STYLE NO. CJ81243
EDITION SIZE: 250, CEL SIZE: 12F
ORIGINAL RETAIL PRICE: $175

STORK NAKED
Warner Bros./Freleng
STYLE NO. N/A
EDITION SIZE: 100, CEL SIZE: 12F
ORIGINAL RETAIL PRICE: $725

MARVIN MARTIAN AND DUCK DODGERS
Warner Bros. Sericels
STYLE NO. N/A
EDITION SIZE: 250, CEL SIZE: 12F
ORIGINAL RETAIL PRICE: $175

MISSISSIPPI HARE
Warner Bros./Jones
STYLE NO. CJ80831
EDITION SIZE: 100, CEL SIZE: 12F
ORIGINAL RETAIL PRICE: $725

SHOWDOWN
Warner Bros. Sericels
STYLE NO. N/A
EDITION SIZE: 250, CEL SIZE: 12F
ORIGINAL RETAIL PRICE: $175

RABBIT SEASONING
Warner Bros./Jones
STYLE NO. CJ80802
EDITION SIZE: 100, CEL SIZE: 12F
ORIGINAL RETAIL PRICE: $750

Image Not Available

SUPER DUCK
Warner Bros. Sericels
STYLE NO. N/A
EDITION SIZE: 250, CEL SIZE: 12F
ORIGINAL RETAIL PRICE: $175

Image Not Available

SYLVESTER AND TWEETY
Warner Bros. Sericels
STYLE NO. N/A
EDITION SIZE: 250, CEL SIZE: 12F
ORIGINAL RETAIL PRICE: $175

TINY TOONS LINE-UP
Warner Bros. Sericels
STYLE NO. N/A
EDITION SIZE: 2500, CEL SIZE: 12F (pan)
ORIGINAL RETAIL PRICE: $275

WILE E. COYOTE AND ROAD RUNNER
Warner Bros. Sericels
STYLE NO. N/A
EDITION SIZE: 250, CEL SIZE: 12F
ORIGINAL RETAIL PRICE: $175

1992

A CORNY CONCERTO
Bob Clampett
STYLE NO. BC1012
EDITION SIZE: 500, CEL SIZE: 16F (pan)
ORIGINAL RETAIL PRICE: $700

BIRDY AND THE BEAST (TITLE)
Bob Clampett
STYLE NO. BC1013
EDITION SIZE: 500, CEL SIZE: 16F (2X)
ORIGINAL RETAIL PRICE: $600

KITTY KORNERED (TITLE)
Bob Clampett
STYLE NO. BC1014
EDITION SIZE: 500, CEL SIZE: 16F (2X)
ORIGINAL RETAIL PRICE: $600

WABBIT TWOUBLE (TITLE)
Bob Clampett
STYLE NO. BC1015
EDITION SIZE: 500, CEL SIZE: 16F (2X)
ORIGINAL RETAIL PRICE: $600

ANTICIPATION
Friz Freleng
STYLE NO. FF1014
EDITION SIZE: 750, CEL SIZE: 16F
ORIGINAL RETAIL PRICE: $555

BABY BUGS
Friz Freleng
STYLE NO. FF1019
EDITION SIZE: 750, CEL SIZE: 12F
ORIGINAL RETAIL PRICE: $550

CAUGHT AGAIN
Friz Freleng
STYLE NO. FF1012
EDITION SIZE: 750, CEL SIZE: 12F
ORIGINAL RETAIL PRICE: $595

PLAY IT AGAIN, SAM
Friz Freleng
STYLE NO. FF1017
EDITION SIZE: 750, CEL SIZE: 16F
ORIGINAL RETAIL PRICE: $675

DIXIE
Friz Freleng
STYLE NO. FF1018
EDITION SIZE: 750, CEL SIZE: 16F
ORIGINAL RETAIL PRICE: $675

SINGING IN THE WAIN
Friz Freleng
STYLE NO. FF1016
EDITION SIZE: 750, CEL SIZE: 16F
ORIGINAL RETAIL PRICE: $1,050

THE DRAW
Friz Freleng
STYLE NO. FF1010
EDITION SIZE: 750, CEL SIZE: 16F
ORIGINAL RETAIL PRICE: $675

TRAVIATA
Friz Freleng
STYLE NO. FF1015
EDITION SIZE: 750, CEL SIZE: 16F
ORIGINAL RETAIL PRICE: $540

A MOUSE DIVIDED
Friz Freleng
STYLE NO. FF1020
EDITION SIZE: 750, CEL SIZE: 16F
ORIGINAL RETAIL PRICE: $600

WHAT'S COOKIN' DOC?
Friz Freleng
STYLE NO. FF1023
EDITION SIZE: 750, CEL SIZE: 16F
ORIGINAL RETAIL PRICE: $675

MUTINY ON THE BUNNY
Friz Freleng
STYLE NO. FF1011
EDITION SIZE: 750, CEL SIZE: 16F
ORIGINAL RETAIL PRICE: $595

ACME ROCKET
Chuck Jones
STYLE NO. CJ80932
EDITION SIZE: 500, CEL SIZE: 12F
ORIGINAL RETAIL PRICE: $550

MY TOWN
Friz Freleng
STYLE NO. FF1013
EDITION SIZE: 750, CEL SIZE: 16F
ORIGINAL RETAIL PRICE: $675

BUGS AND WITCH HAZEL (II)
Chuck Jones
STYLE NO. CJ80992
EDITION SIZE: 500, CEL SIZE: 16F
ORIGINAL RETAIL PRICE: $550

BUGS AND GULLI-BULL (III)
Chuck Jones
STYLE NO. CJ81022
EDITION SIZE: 500, CEL SIZE: 16F
ORIGINAL RETAIL PRICE: $750

CHEERS!
Chuck Jones
STYLE NO. CJ81053
EDITION SIZE: 500, CEL SIZE: 12F
ORIGINAL RETAIL PRICE: $600

FRIGID HARE
Chuck Jones
STYLE NO. CJ80962
EDITION SIZE: 500, CEL SIZE: 12F
ORIGINAL RETAIL PRICE: $550

HAREDRESSER
Chuck Jones
STYLE NO. CJ80952
EDITION SIZE: 500, CEL SIZE: 12F
ORIGINAL RETAIL PRICE: $550

HOME SWEET HOME
Chuck Jones
STYLE NO. CJ81001
EDITION SIZE: 750, CEL SIZE: 16F
ORIGINAL RETAIL PRICE: $500

NEW YORKER BUGS
Chuck Jones
STYLE NO. CJ80941
EDITION SIZE: 100, CEL SIZE: 12F (pan)
ORIGINAL RETAIL PRICE: $600

ROMEO AND JULIET
Chuck Jones
STYLE NO. CJ81012
EDITION SIZE: 500, CEL SIZE: 16F (pan)
ORIGINAL RETAIL PRICE: $1,400

SAND TROPEZ BUNNY
Chuck Jones
STYLE NO. CJ81031
EDITION SIZE: 500, CEL SIZE: 12F
ORIGINAL RETAIL PRICE: $500

SHERWOOD FOREST GROUP
Chuck Jones
STYLE NO. CJ80989
EDITION SIZE: 500, CEL SIZE: 16F
ORIGINAL RETAIL PRICE: $1,200

SHOWDOWN
Chuck Jones
STYLE NO. CJ80972
EDITION SIZE: 500, CEL SIZE: 16F
ORIGINAL RETAIL PRICE: $750

TOO CLEAN FOR COMFORT
Chuck Jones
STYLE NO. CJ26857
EDITION SIZE: 500, CEL SIZE: 12F
ORIGINAL RETAIL PRICE: $550

WED WIVER VAHWEE
Chuck Jones
STYLE NO. CJ8091A
EDITION SIZE: 750, CEL SIZE: 16F
ORIGINAL RETAIL PRICE: $950

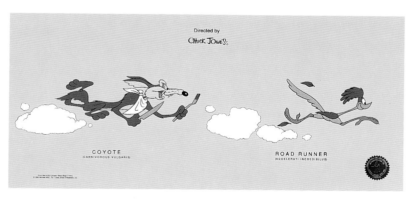

BEEP, BEEP!
Chuck Jones Sericels
STYLE NO. SC00003
EDITION SIZE: 9,500, CEL SIZE: 16F
  (pan)
ORIGINAL RETAIL PRICE: $155

BULLY FOR BUGS
Chuck Jones Sericels
STYLE NO. SC00004
EDITION SIZE: 9,500, CEL SIZE: 16F
  (pan)
ORIGINAL RETAIL PRICE: $145

FIGARO FERTILIZER
Chuck Jones Sericels
STYLE NO. SC00001
EDITION SIZE: 9,500, CEL SIZE: 16F+
ORIGINAL RETAIL PRICE: $160

FOR SCENT-IMENTAL REASONS
Chuck Jones Sericels
STYLE NO. SC00002
EDITION SIZE: 9,500, CEL SIZE: 16F+
ORIGINAL RETAIL PRICE: $120

BASH BROTHERS?
Robert McKimson
STYLE NO. BM1007
EDITION SIZE: 250, CEL SIZE: 12F
ORIGINAL RETAIL PRICE: $575

DOCTORING DAFFY: CHICAGO CUBS
Robert McKimson
STYLE NO. BM1011
EDITION SIZE: 250, CEL SIZE: 12F
ORIGINAL RETAIL PRICE: $625

DODGER BUGS
Robert McKimson
STYLE NO. BM2007
EDITION SIZE: 300, CEL SIZE: 12F
ORIGINAL RETAIL PRICE: $575

SUPPERTIME
Robert McKimson
STYLE NO. BM1004
EDITION SIZE: 750, CEL SIZE: 12F
ORIGINAL RETAIL PRICE: $750

HOME RUN HARE: NEW YORK YANKEES
Robert McKimson
STYLE NO. BM1010
EDITION SIZE: 250, CEL SIZE: 12F
ORIGINAL RETAIL PRICE: $625

TAZ RIPPED
Robert McKimson
STYLE NO. BM1003
EDITION SIZE: 250, CEL SIZE: 12F
ORIGINAL RETAIL PRICE: $560

I TAWT I TAGGED A PUDDY TAT
Robert McKimson
STYLE NO. BM1001
EDITION SIZE: 250, CEL SIZE: 12F
ORIGINAL RETAIL PRICE: $625

YER OUT!
Robert McKimson
STYLE NO. BM100
EDITION SIZE: 250, CEL SIZE: 12F
ORIGINAL RETAIL PRICE: $625

NUMBER ONE GOLFER
Robert McKimson
STYLE NO. BM9938
EDITION SIZE: 300, CEL SIZE: 12F
ORIGINAL RETAIL PRICE: $550

YOU MAKE THE CALL: MILWAUKEE
    BREWERS
Robert McKimson
STYLE NO. BM1009
EDITION SIZE: 250, CEL SIZE: 12F
ORIGINAL RETAIL PRICE: $575

RED HOT: CINCINNATI REDS
Robert McKimson
STYLE NO. BM1008
EDITION SIZE: 250, CEL SIZE: 12F
ORIGINAL RETAIL PRICE: $575

YOU SNOOZE, YOU LOSE
Robert McKimson
STYLE NO. BM1013
EDITION SIZE: 500, CEL SIZE: 12F
ORIGINAL RETAIL PRICE: $550

THE SQUEEZE
Robert McKimson
STYLE NO. BM1002
EDITION SIZE: 250, CEL SIZE: 12F
ORIGINAL RETAIL PRICE: $575

1991 NATIONAL LEAGUE CHAMPS:
    ATLANTA BRAVES
Robert McKimson
STYLE NO. BM1005
EDITION SIZE: 250, CEL SIZE: 12F
ORIGINAL RETAIL PRICE: $700

1991 WORLD CHAMPS: MINNESOTA
  TWINS
Robert McKimson
STYLE NO. BM1006
EDITION SIZE: 250, CEL SIZE: 12F
ORIGINAL RETAIL PRICE: $800

SNOWSHOE BUGS
Robert McKimson Sericels
STYLE NO. N/A
EDITION SIZE: 7,500, CEL SIZE: 12F
ORIGINAL RETAIL PRICE: $190

ARIBA! ARIBA!
Robert McKimson Sericels
STYLE NO. N/A
EDITION SIZE: 7,500, CEL SIZE: 12F
ORIGINAL RETAIL PRICE: $190

TAZ
Robert McKimson Sericels
STYLE NO. N/A
EDITION SIZE: 7,500, CEL SIZE: 12F
ORIGINAL RETAIL PRICE: $190

BASEBALL BUGS
Robert McKimson Sericels
STYLE NO. N/A
EDITION SIZE: 7,500, CEL SIZE: 12F
ORIGINAL RETAIL PRICE: $190

JAZZ PLAYER
Virgil Ross
STYLE NO. VR100
EDITION SIZE: 500, CEL SIZE: 16F
ORIGINAL RETAIL PRICE: $600

LIKE FATHER, LIKE SON
Robert McKimson Sericels
STYLE NO. N/A
EDITION SIZE: 7,500, CEL SIZE: 12F
ORIGINAL RETAIL PRICE: $190

NO MORE PIDDIES
Virgil Ross
STYLE NO. VR400
EDITION SIZE: 500, CEL SIZE: 16F (pan)
ORIGINAL RETAIL PRICE: $700

LOADED HANDS
Robert McKimson Sericels
STYLE NO. N/A
EDITION SIZE: 7,500, CEL SIZE: 12F
ORIGINAL RETAIL PRICE: $190

THE POUNCE
Virgil Ross
STYLE NO. VR300
EDITION SIZE: 500, CEL SIZE: 16F
ORIGINAL RETAIL PRICE: $600

TWEETY'S GWEAT ESCAPE
Virgil Ross
STYLE NO. VR400
EDITION SIZE: 500, CEL SIZE: 16F
ORIGINAL RETAIL PRICE: $600

PILOT BUGS
Warner Bros. Sericels
STYLE NO. SC1040
EDITION SIZE: 2,500, CEL SIZE: 12F
ORIGINAL RETAIL PRICE: $175

WRONG NUMBER
Virgil Ross
STYLE NO. VR200
EDITION SIZE: 500, CEL SIZE: 16F
ORIGINAL RETAIL PRICE: $600

TEED OFF
Warner Bros. Sericels
STYLE NO. SC1048
EDITION SIZE: 2,500, CEL SIZE: 12F
ORIGINAL RETAIL PRICE: $175

AIR AND HARE
Warner Bros. Limited Editions
STYLE NO. WB1000
EDITION SIZE: 250, CEL SIZE: 12F
ORIGINAL RETAIL PRICE: $750

1993

THE BIG SNOOZE
Bob Clampett
STYLE NO. BC1017
EDITION SIZE: 500, CEL SIZE: 16F
ORIGINAL RETAIL PRICE: $550

ANYONE FOR TENNIS?
Warner Bros./Freleng
STYLE NO. N/A
EDITION SIZE: N/A, CEL SIZE: 12F
ORIGINAL RETAIL PRICE: N/A

GOT HIM
Friz Freleng
STYLE NO. FF1025
EDITION SIZE: 750, CEL SIZE: 16F
ORIGINAL RETAIL PRICE: $850

ANCHORS AWEIGH
Warner Bros. Sericels
STYLE NO. SC1039
EDITION SIZE: 2,500, CEL SIZE: 12F
ORIGINAL RETAIL PRICE: $175

SAHARA SAM
Friz Freleng
STYLE NO. FF1024
EDITION SIZE: 750, CEL SIZE: 16F+
ORIGINAL RETAIL PRICE: $950

MICHIGAN J. FROG
Warner Bros. Sericels
STYLE NO. N/A
EDITION SIZE: 2,500, CEL SIZE: 12F
ORIGINAL RETAIL PRICE: $175

ACME BIRD SEED
Chuck Jones
STYLE NO. CJ81151
EDITION SIZE: 500, CEL SIZE: 12F
ORIGINAL RETAIL PRICE: $1,200

AIN'T I A STINKER?
Chuck Jones
STYLE NO. CJ81252
EDITION SIZE: 500, CEL SIZE: 16F
ORIGINAL RETAIL PRICE: $675

BUGS AND GULLI-BULL
Chuck Jones
STYLE NO. CJ81222
EDITION SIZE: 750, CEL SIZE: 16F
ORIGINAL RETAIL PRICE: $850

DAFFY BEAKHEAD
Chuck Jones
STYLE NO. CJ81122
EDITION SIZE: 500, CEL SIZE: 16F
ORIGINAL RETAIL PRICE: $550

DETHPICABLE COURTROOM
Chuck Jones
STYLE NO. CJ81083
EDITION SIZE: 500, CEL SIZE: 12F
ORIGINAL RETAIL PRICE: $600

DUCK DODGERS: FINALE
Chuck Jones
STYLE NO. CJ81163
EDITION SIZE: 500, CEL SIZE: 16F (pan)
ORIGINAL RETAIL PRICE: $1,400

DYNAMITE HARE
Chuck Jones
STYLE NO. CJ81142
EDITION SIZE: 500, CEL SIZE: 12F
ORIGINAL RETAIL PRICE: $600

I GIVE UP SEASON
Chuck Jones
STYLE NO. CJ81113
EDITION SIZE: 500, CEL SIZE: 16F
ORIGINAL RETAIL PRICE: $800

MARK OF ZERO
Chuck Jones
STYLE NO. CJ81235
EDITION SIZE: 750, CEL SIZE: 16F
ORIGINAL RETAIL PRICE: $1,000

PEWLITZER PRIZE
Chuck Jones
STYLE NO. CJ81301
EDITION SIZE: 750, CEL SIZE: 12F
ORIGINAL RETAIL PRICE: $550

RABBIT OF SEVILLE (III)
Chuck Jones
STYLE NO. CJ81282
EDITION SIZE: 750, CEL SIZE: 16F
ORIGINAL RETAIL PRICE: $600

18TH HARE
Chuck Jones
STYLE NO. CJ81132
EDITION SIZE: 500, CEL SIZE: 16F
ORIGINAL RETAIL PRICE: $550

ROAD SCHOLAR
Chuck Jones
STYLE NO. CJ81062
EDITION SIZE: 500, CEL SIZE: 12F
ORIGINAL RETAIL PRICE: $550

BUGS AND HONEY BUNNY
Robert McKimson
STYLE NO. BM1014
EDITION SIZE: 500 CEL SIZE: 12F
ORIGINAL RETAIL PRICE: $550

SHE IS SHY
Chuck Jones
STYLE NO. CJ81172
EDITION SIZE: 500, CEL SIZE: 12F
ORIGINAL RETAIL PRICE: $600

GORILLA MY DREAMS
Robert McKimson
STYLE NO. BM0091
EDITION SIZE: 750, CEL SIZE: 16F
ORIGINAL RETAIL PRICE: $750

SOUND PLEASE
Chuck Jones
STYLE NO. CJ81291
EDITION SIZE: 500, CEL SIZE: 12F
ORIGINAL RETAIL PRICE: $600

GROUCHO BUGS
Robert McKimson
STYLE NO. BM2006
EDITION SIZE: 500, CEL SIZE: 12F
ORIGINAL RETAIL PRICE: $550

WHAT'S OPERA, DOC? (IV)
Chuck Jones
STYLE NO. CJ81192
EDITION SIZE: 750, CEL SIZE: 16F
ORIGINAL RETAIL PRICE: $850

GROUNDHOG'S DAY
Robert McKimson
STYLE NO. BM2020
EDITION SIZE: 500, CEL SIZE: 12F
ORIGINAL RETAIL PRICE: $560

HOW MANY LUMPS?
Robert McKimson
STYLE NO. BM2013
EDITION SIZE: 500, CEL SIZE: 16F
ORIGINAL RETAIL PRICE: $750

I Say, I Say, Son . . .
Robert McKimson
STYLE NO. BM2014
EDITION SIZE: 500, CEL SIZE: 12F
ORIGINAL RETAIL PRICE: $560

Who-o-a!
Virgil Ross
STYLE NO. VR100WB
EDITION SIZE: 500, CEL SIZE: 16F
ORIGINAL RETAIL PRICE: $600

Gunslingers
Virgil Ross
STYLE NO. VR700
EDITION SIZE: 500, CEL SIZE: 16F (pan)
ORIGINAL RETAIL PRICE: $900

A Wild Hare
Virgil Ross
STYLE NO. VR800
EDITION SIZE: 500, CEL SIZE: 12F
ORIGINAL RETAIL PRICE: $600

Look, I'm Dancing!
Virgil Ross
STYLE NO. N/A
EDITION SIZE: 750, CEL SIZE: 16F (pan)
ORIGINAL RETAIL PRICE: $800

The Heckling Hare
Warner Bros./Avery
STYLE NO. TA1001
EDITION SIZE: 500, CEL SIZE: 16F
ORIGINAL RETAIL PRICE: $550

Show Stoppers
Virgil Ross
STYLE NO. VR600
EDITION SIZE: 500, CEL SIZE: 16F
ORIGINAL RETAIL PRICE: $700

Aerospace Jordan
Warner Bros. Limited Editions
STYLE NO. WB1002
EDITION SIZE: 500, CEL SIZE: 12F
ORIGINAL RETAIL PRICE: $750

Tropical Hare
Virgil Ross
STYLE NO. VR900
EDITION SIZE: 500, CEL SIZE: 12F
ORIGINAL RETAIL PRICE: $700

Be A Clown
Warner Bros. Limited Editions
STYLE NO. WB1005
EDITION SIZE: 500, CEL SIZE: 16F
ORIGINAL RETAIL PRICE: $425

THE CAT AND THE CLAW
Warner Bros. Limited Editions
STYLE NO. WB1004
EDITION SIZE: 500, CEL SIZE: 16F
ORIGINAL RETAIL PRICE: $425

TINY TOONS WESTERN
Warner Bros. Sericels
STYLE NO. SC1006
EDITION SIZE: 2,500, CEL SIZE: 12F
ORIGINAL RETAIL PRICE: $175

I AM THE NIGHT
Warner Bros. Limited Editions
STYLE NO. WB1003
EDITION SIZE: 500, CEL SIZE: 12F
ORIGINAL RETAIL PRICE: $350

1994

BUGS PERSONA
Bob Clampett
STYLE NO. BC1018
EDITION SIZE: 750, CEL SIZE: 16F
ORIGINAL RETAIL PRICE: $525

LOONEY TUNES ON PARADE
Warner Bros. Limited Editions
STYLE NO. WB1006
EDITION SIZE: 750, CEL SIZE: 16F (pan)
ORIGINAL RETAIL PRICE: $950

MY HERO
Bob Clampett
STYLE NO. BC1019
EDITION SIZE: 500, CEL SIZE: 12F
ORIGINAL RETAIL PRICE: $500

DYNAMITE DIAGNOSIS
Warner Bros. Sericels
STYLE NO. SC1043
EDITION SIZE: 2,500, CEL SIZE: 12F
ORIGINAL RETAIL PRICE: $175

THE BIG SNEEZE
Friz Freleng
STYLE NO. FF1035
EDITION SIZE: 750, CEL SIZE: 16F
ORIGINAL RETAIL PRICE: $700

NO SPRING CHICKEN
Friz Freleng
STYLE NO. FF1039A
EDITION SIZE: 250, CEL SIZE: 12F
ORIGINAL RETAIL PRICE: $625

TAZ MOTORCYCLE
Warner Bros. Sericels
STYLE NO. SC1042
EDITION SIZE: 2,500, CEL SIZE: 12F
ORIGINAL RETAIL PRICE: $175

PAR FOR THE COURSE
Friz Freleng
STYLE NO. FF1027
EDITION SIZE: 750, CEL SIZE: 12F
ORIGINAL RETAIL PRICE: $625

ACME HARPOON GUN
Chuck Jones
STYLE NO. CJ81412
EDITION SIZE: 750, CEL SIZE: 16F
ORIGINAL RETAIL PRICE: $950

RIDE 'EM SAM
Friz Freleng
STYLE NO. FF1033
EDITION SIZE: 750, CEL SIZE: 16F
ORIGINAL RETAIL PRICE: $650

BUGS (TITLE)
Chuck Jones
STYLE NO. CJ81391
EDITION SIZE: 750, CEL SIZE: 16F
ORIGINAL RETAIL PRICE: $850

THE SHOWDOWN
Friz Freleng
STYLE NO. FF1037
EDITION SIZE: 750, CEL SIZE: 12F
ORIGINAL RETAIL PRICE: $625

CURTAIN CALL
Chuck Jones
STYLE NO. CJ81352
EDITION SIZE: 500, CEL SIZE: 16F
ORIGINAL RETAIL PRICE: $600

SYLVESTER'S BUFFET
Friz Freleng
STYLE NO. FF1036
EDITION SIZE: 750, CEL SIZE: 12F
ORIGINAL RETAIL PRICE: $650

EVOLUTION OF DAFFY
Chuck Jones
STYLE NO. CJ81317
EDITION SIZE: 500, CEL SIZE: 16F (pan)
ORIGINAL RETAIL PRICE: $1,525

THE TWO MUSKETEERS
Friz Freleng
STYLE NO. FF1038
EDITION SIZE: 750, CEL SIZE: 16F
ORIGINAL RETAIL PRICE: $700

MICHIGAN J. FROG (VI)
Chuck Jones
STYLE NO. CJ81461
EDITION SIZE: 750, CEL SIZE: 12F
ORIGINAL RETAIL PRICE: $650

PEACE AND CARROTS
Chuck Jones
STYLE NO. CJ81532
EDITION SIZE: 750, CEL SIZE: 16F
ORIGINAL RETAIL PRICE: $950

PLANET X
Chuck Jones
STYLE NO. CJ81342
EDITION SIZE: 750, CEL SIZE: 16F
ORIGINAL RETAIL PRICE: $950

PRINCE'S BRIDE
Chuck Jones
STYLE NO. CJ81522
EDITION SIZE: 500, CEL SIZE: 12F
ORIGINAL RETAIL PRICE: $675

LE PURSUIT
Chuck Jones
STYLE NO. CJ81442
EDITION SIZE: 750, CEL SIZE: 12F (2X)
ORIGINAL RETAIL PRICE: $1,325

RABBIT OF SEVILLE (IV)
Chuck Jones
STYLE NO. CJ81402
EDITION SIZE: 500, CEL SIZE: 16F
ORIGINAL RETAIL PRICE: N/A

ROCKET SQUAD
Chuck Jones
STYLE NO. CJ81452
EDITION SIZE: 500, CEL SIZE: 12F
ORIGINAL RETAIL PRICE: $675

 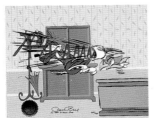

SAY AHHH . . .
Chuck Jones
STYLE NO. CJ81362
EDITION SIZE: 750, CEL SIZE: 12F (2X)
ORIGINAL RETAIL PRICE: $1,325

SUSPENDED ANIMATION
Chuck Jones
STYLE NO. CJ81382
EDITION SIZE: 750, CEL SIZE: 12F
ORIGINAL RETAIL PRICE: $675

TRUANT OFFICER
Chuck Jones
STYLE NO. CJ81324
EDITION SIZE: 750, CEL SIZE: 16F
ORIGINAL RETAIL PRICE: $950

TURNABOUT IS FAIR PLAY
Chuck Jones
STYLE NO. CJ81332
EDITION SIZE: 750, CEL SIZE: 16F
ORIGINAL RETAIL PRICE: $950

TWO PAIR HARE
Chuck Jones
STYLE NO. CJ81592
EDITION SIZE: 350, CEL SIZE: 12F
ORIGINAL RETAIL PRICE: $675

HOOKED ON TWEETY
Virgil Ross
STYLE NO. VR1100
EDITION SIZE: 500, CEL SIZE: 16F (pan)
ORIGINAL RETAIL PRICE: $895

HILLBILLY HARE
Robert McKimson
STYLE NO. BM1001
EDITION SIZE: 250, CEL SIZE: 16F
ORIGINAL RETAIL PRICE: $500

LITTLE RED RIDING RABBIT
Virgil Ross
STYLE NO. VR1300
EDITION SIZE: 500, CEL SIZE: 16F
ORIGINAL RETAIL PRICE: $795

STRIKE UP THE BAND
Robert McKimson
STYLE NO. BM0093
EDITION SIZE: 750, CEL SIZE: 16F (pan)
ORIGINAL RETAIL PRICE: $950

SCUSE ME, PARDON ME
Virgil Ross
STYLE NO. VR1400
EDITION SIZE: 750, CEL SIZE: 12F (pan)
ORIGINAL RETAIL PRICE: $895

TIMBER!
Virgil Ross
STYLE NO. VR1500
EDITION SIZE: 750, CEL SIZE: 12F (pan)
ORIGINAL RETAIL PRICE: $875

HIGH DIVING SAM
Virgil Ross
STYLE NO. VR1200
EDITION SIZE: 750, CEL SIZE: 12F (pan)
ORIGINAL RETAIL PRICE: $895

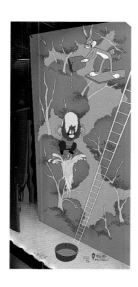

YER OUT!
Virgil Ross
STYLE NO. VR1000
EDITION SIZE: 750, CEL SIZE: 16F (pan)
ORIGINAL RETAIL PRICE: $895

DAFFY DUCK IN HOLLYWOOD
Warner Bros./Avery
STYLE NO. TA1002
EDITION SIZE: 250, CEL SIZE: 12F
ORIGINAL RETAIL PRICE: $500

BIRDS ANONYMOUS
Warner Bros./Freleng
STYLE NO. FF1034
EDITION SIZE: 750, CEL SIZE: 12F
ORIGINAL RETAIL PRICE: $725

AEROSPACE JORDAN (II):
    THAT'S ALL FOLKS!
Warner Bros. Limited Editions
STYLE NO. WB1007
EDITION SIZE: 750, CEL SIZE: 16F (pan)
ORIGINAL RETAIL PRICE: $950

HARLEY TOYS WITH BATMAN
Warner Bros. Limited Editions
STYLE NO. WB1009
EDITION SIZE: 500, CEL SIZE: 12F
ORIGINAL RETAIL PRICE: $350

INSIDE THE WATER TOWER
Warner Bros. Limited Editions
STYLE NO. WB1011
EDITION SIZE: 750, CEL SIZE: 16F (pan)
ORIGINAL RETAIL PRICE: $650

TAZ MODEL SHEET
Warner Bros. Limited Editions
STYLE NO. WB1008
EDITION SIZE: 750, CEL SIZE: 16F
ORIGINAL RETAIL PRICE: $525

A TOUCH OF POISON IVY
Warner Bros. Limited Editions
STYLE NO. WB1010
EDITION SIZE: 500, CEL SIZE: 16F
ORIGINAL RETAIL PRICE: $425

BATMAN AND ROBIN
Warner Bros. Sericels
STYLE NO. SC1008
EDITION SIZE: 5,000, CEL SIZE: 12F
ORIGINAL RETAIL PRICE: $175

VILLAINS OF GOTHAM CITY
Warner Bros. Sericels
STYLE NO. SC1007
EDITION SIZE: 5,000, CEL SIZE: 12F
  (pan)
ORIGINAL RETAIL PRICE: $275

COYOTE FALLING
Warner Bros. Sericels
STYLE NO. SC1014
EDITION SIZE: 1,000, CEL SIZE: 12F
  (dim)
ORIGINAL RETAIL PRICE: $275

FEED THE KITTY
Warner Bros. Sericels
STYLE NO. SC1012
EDITION SIZE: 2,500, CEL SIZE: 12F
ORIGINAL RETAIL PRICE: $175

HARE DO
Warner Bros. Sericels
STYLE NO. SC1009
EDITION SIZE: 5,000, CEL SIZE:12F
ORIGINAL RETAIL PRICE: $175

CHICKEN TONIGHT
Friz Freleng
STYLE NO. FF1042
EDITION SIZE: 500, CEL SIZE: 12F
ORIGINAL RETAIL PRICE: $625

PUDDY TATS CAN'T FLY
Warner Bros. Sericels
STYLE NO. SC1013
EDITION SIZE: 1,000, CEL SIZE: 12F
   (dim)
ORIGINAL RETAIL PRICE: $275

IT'S A GRAND OL' FLAG
Friz Freleng
STYLE NO. FF1043
EDITION SIZE: 250, CEL SIZE: 12F
ORIGINAL RETAIL PRICE: $625

SPECIAL DELIVERY FROM MARS
Warner Bros. Sericels
STYLE NO. SC1011
EDITION SIZE: 5,000, CEL SIZE: 12F
ORIGINAL RETAIL PRICE: $175

MEXICAN CAT DANCE
Friz Freleng
STYLE NO. FF1041
EDITION SIZE: 500, CEL SIZE: 12F
ORIGINAL RETAIL PRICE: $625

TENNIS, ANYONE?
Warner Bros. Sericels
STYLE NO. SC1010
EDITION SIZE: 5,000, CEL SIZE: 12F
ORIGINAL RETAIL PRICE: $175

PALOOKA PITCH
Friz Freleng
STYLE NO. FF1040
EDITION SIZE: 500, CEL SIZE: 12F
ORIGINAL RETAIL PRICE: $625

1995

PROCESS OF ANIMATION
Bob Clampett
STYLE NO. BC1020
EDITION SIZE: 500, CEL SIZE: 12F (pan)
ORIGINAL RETAIL PRICE: $650

BUGS & CRUSHER
Chuck Jones
STYLE NO. CJ81612
EDITION SIZE: 500, CEL SIZE: 12F
ORIGINAL RETAIL PRICE: $675

CHARIOTS OF FUR
Chuck Jones
STYLE NO. CJ81632
EDITION SIZE: 500, CEL SIZE: 12F
ORIGINAL RETAIL PRICE: $675

FISH TALE
Chuck Jones
STYLE NO. CJ81622
EDITION SIZE: 500, CEL SIZE: 12F
ORIGINAL RETAIL PRICE: $625

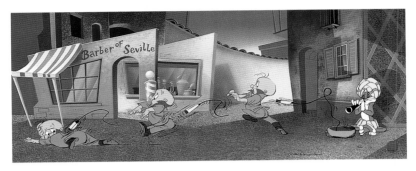

RABBIT OF SEVILLE (V)
Chuck Jones
STYLE NO. CJ81744
EDITION SIZE: N/A, CEL SIZE: 16F (pan)
ORIGINAL RETAIL PRICE: N/A

INSTANT MARTIANS
Chuck Jones
STYLE NO. CJ81693
EDITION SIZE: 750, CEL SIZE: 12F
ORIGINAL RETAIL PRICE: $725

RUDE JESTER
Chuck Jones
STYLE NO. CJ81602
EDITION SIZE: 500, CEL SIZE: 12F
ORIGINAL RETAIL PRICE: $625

METER LEADER
Chuck Jones
STYLE NO. CJ81751
EDITION SIZE: 500, CEL SIZE: 12F
ORIGINAL RETAIL PRICE: $675

SANTA ON TRIAL
Chuck Jones
STYLE NO. CJ81653
EDITION SIZE: 500, CEL SIZE: 12F
ORIGINAL RETAIL PRICE: $725

NASTY CANASTA
Chuck Jones
STYLE NO. CJ81732
EDITION SIZE: 500, CEL SIZE: 12F
ORIGINAL RETAIL PRICE: $675

KABOOM
Virgil Ross
STYLE NO. VR1600
EDITION SIZE: 750, CEL SIZE: 16F (pan)
ORIGINAL RETAIL PRICE: $995

LOONEY BIN
Virgil Ross
STYLE NO. VR1700
EDITION SIZE: 750, CEL SIZE: 16F+
ORIGINAL RETAIL PRICE: $1895

PEPÉ'S 50TH BIRTHDAY
Chuck Jones
STYLE NO. CJ81682
EDITION SIZE: 400, CEL SIZE: 16F
ORIGINAL RETAIL PRICE: $1025

MINESHAFT SHUFFLE
Virgil Ross
STYLE NO. VR1700A
EDITION SIZE: 500, CEL SIZE: 16F (pan)
ORIGINAL RETAIL PRICE: $995

SCARED HARE
Virgil Ross
STYLE NO. VR1702
EDITION SIZE: 500, CEL SIZE: 16F (pan)
ORIGINAL RETAIL PRICE: $995

ALMOST GOT 'IM
Warner Bros. Limited Editions
STYLE NO. WB1015
EDITION SIZE: 500, CEL SIZE: 16F
ORIGINAL RETAIL PRICE: $600

CARROTBLANCA
Warner Bros. Limited Editions
STYLE NO. WB1023
EDITION SIZE: 250, CEL SIZE: 12F
ORIGINAL RETAIL PRICE: $450

DAFFY PERSONA
Warner Bros. Limited Editions
STYLE NO. WB1020
EDITION SIZE: 750, CEL SIZE: 16F
ORIGINAL RETAIL PRICE: $525

THE GREAT SPACE ERASE
Warner Bros. Limited Editions
STYLE NO. WB1017
EDITION SIZE: 750, CEL SIZE: 16F
ORIGINAL RETAIL PRICE: $1750

HEART OF ICE
Warner Bros. Limited Editions
STYLE NO. WB1022
EDITION SIZE: 500, CEL SIZE: 16F
ORIGINAL RETAIL PRICE: $475

HELLO NURSE
Warner Bros. Limited Editions
STYLE NO. WB1018
EDITION SIZE: 500, CEL SIZE: 12F
ORIGINAL RETAIL PRICE: $425

THE GREAT ONES
Warner Bros. Limited Editions
STYLE NO. WB1021
EDITION SIZE: 750, CEL SIZE: 16F
ORIGINAL RETAIL PRICE: $1,250

MARK OF A QUESTION
Warner Bros. Limited Editions
STYLE NO. WB1013
EDITION SIZE: 500, CEL SIZE: 12F
ORIGINAL RETAIL PRICE: $350

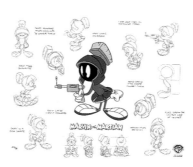

MARVIN MARTIAN MODEL SHEET
Warner Bros. Limited Editions
STYLE NO. WB1024
EDITION SIZE: 750, CEL SIZE: 16F
ORIGINAL RETAIL PRICE: $525

MICHIGAN J. FROG MODEL SHEET
Warner Bros. Limited Editions
STYLE NO. WB1014
EDITION SIZE: 750, CEL SIZE: 16F
ORIGINAL RETAIL PRICE: $525

NO FREE CHEESE
Warner Bros. Limited Editions
STYLE NO. WB1019
EDITION SIZE: 500, CEL SIZE: 12F
ORIGINAL RETAIL PRICE: $400

PINKY AND THE BRAIN
Warner Bros. Limited Editions
STYLE NO. WB1012
EDITION SIZE: 500, CEL SIZE: 12F
ORIGINAL RETAIL PRICE: $350

KNIGHT MOVES
Warner Bros. Sericels
STYLE NO. SC1017
EDITION SIZE: 1,000, CEL SIZE: 12F(dim)
ORIGINAL RETAIL PRICE: $275

WE ARE THE TOONS
Warner Bros. Limited Editions
STYLE NO. WB1016
EDITION SIZE: 750, CEL SIZE: 16F(pan)
ORIGINAL RETAIL PRICE: $975

13TH HOLE
Warner Bros. Sericels
STYLE NO. SC1018
EDITION SIZE: 2,500, CEL SIZE: 12F
ORIGINAL RETAIL PRICE: $175

LOONEY LINE-UP
Warner Bros. Sericels
STYLE NO. SC1023
EDITION SIZE: 7,500, CEL SIZE: 16F(pan)
ORIGINAL RETAIL PRICE: $425

OF MICE AND MANIACS
Warner Bros. Sericels
STYLE NO. SC1020
EDITION SIZE: 2,500, CEL SIZE: 12F
ORIGINAL RETAIL PRICE: $175

ACME HYPNOTIST
Warner Bros. Sericels
STYLE NO. SC1022
EDITION SIZE: 2,500, CEL SIZE: 12F
ORIGINAL RETAIL PRICE: $175

BARNYARD BULLY
Warner Bros. Sericels
STYLE NO. SC1024
EDITION SIZE: 2,500, CEL SIZE: 12F(pan)
ORIGINAL RETAIL PRICE: $185

"RIBET"
Warner Bros. Sericels
STYLE NO. SC1021
EDITION SIZE: 2,500, CEL SIZE: 12F
ORIGINAL RETAIL PRICE: $175

DUCK AMUCK
Warner Bros. Sericels
STYLE NO. SC1019
EDITION SIZE: 1,000, CEL SIZE:
12F(dim)
ORIGINAL RETAIL PRICE: $275

SYLVESTER UNPLUGGED
Warner Bros. Sericels
STYLE NO. SC1016
EDITION SIZE: 2,500, CEL SIZE: 12F
ORIGINAL RETAIL PRICE: $175

TILL DEATH DO US PART
Warner Bros. Sericels
STYLE NO. SC1015
EDITION SIZE: 2,500, CEL SIZE: 12F
ORIGINAL RETAIL PRICE: $175

VILLAINS OF GOTHAM CITY (II)
Warner Bros. Sericels
STYLE NO. SC1031
EDITION SIZE: 2500, CEL SIZE: 12F(pan)
ORIGINAL RETAIL PRICE: $275

1996

BUGS MIRANDA
Bob Clampett
STYLE NO. BC1021
EDITION SIZE: 500, CEL SIZE: 16F
ORIGINAL RETAIL PRICE: $750

ABOMINABLE SNOW BUNNY
Chuck Jones
STYLE NO. CJ81812
EDITION SIZE: 500, CEL SIZE: 12F
ORIGINAL RETAIL PRICE: $675

SLUGGERS
Robert McKimson
STYLE NO. N/A
EDITION SIZE: 2500, CEL SIZE: 16F
ORIGINAL RETAIL PRICE: N/A

BUGS AND THUGS
Virgil Ross
STYLE NO. VR1704
EDITION SIZE: 500, CEL SIZE: 12F
ORIGINAL RETAIL PRICE: $525

THE LAST CLAW
Virgil Ross
STYLE NO. VR1703
EDITION SIZE: 500, CEL SIZE: 16F(pan)
ORIGINAL RETAIL PRICE: $625

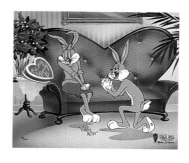

WILL YA?
Virgil Ross
STYLE NO. VR1701
EDITION SIZE: 500, CEL SIZE: 12F
ORIGINAL RETAIL PRICE: $625

BOWERY BUGS
Warner Bros./Davis
STYLE NO. WB1034
EDITION SIZE: 500, CEL SIZE: 12.5F
ORIGINAL RETAIL PRICE: $525

BAD OL' PUDDY TAT
Warner Bros./Freleng
STYLE NO. FF1044
EDITION SIZE: 500, CEL SIZE: 12F
ORIGINAL RETAIL PRICE: $6

BALONEY IN OUR SLACKS
Warner Bros. Limited Editions
STYLE NO. WB1031
EDITION SIZE: 500, CEL SIZE: 12F
ORIGINAL RETAIL PRICE: $425

BATMAN MODEL SHEET
Warner Bros. Limited Editions
STYLE NO. WB1041
EDITION SIZE: 500, CEL SIZE: 16F
ORIGINAL RETAIL PRICE: $525

CATCH THE BIRDIE
Warner Bros. Limited Editions
STYLE NO. WB1030
EDITION SIZE: 750, CEL SIZE: 16F
ORIGINAL RETAIL PRICE: $1250

C'EST FINI
Warner Bros. Limited Editions
STYLE NO. WB1051
EDITION SIZE: 500, CEL SIZE: 12F
ORIGINAL RETAIL PRICE: $500

CHEZ BUGS
Warner Bros. Limited Editions
STYLE NO. WB1036
EDITION SIZE: 250, CEL SIZE: 12F
ORIGINAL RETAIL PRICE: $450

DYNAMIC DUO
Warner Bros. Limited Editions
STYLE NO. WB1038
EDITION SIZE: 500, CEL SIZE: 16F
ORIGINAL RETAIL PRICE: $475

FORE! . . . FIVE! . . .
Warner Bros. Limited Editions
STYLE NO. WB1032
EDITION SIZE: 750, CEL SIZE: 16F
ORIGINAL RETAIL PRICE: $1750

GIRLS' NIGHT OUT
Warner Bros. Limited Editions
STYLE NO. WB1027
EDITION SIZE: 500, CEL SIZE: 12F
ORIGINAL RETAIL PRICE: $425

THE GREATEST
Warner Bros. Limited Editions
STYLE NO. WB1039
EDITION SIZE: 350, CEL SIZE: 16F
ORIGINAL RETAIL PRICE: $950

HARLEY QUINN MODEL SHEET
Warner Bros. Limited Editions
STYLE NO. WB1050
EDITION SIZE: 500, CEL SIZE: 16F
ORIGINAL RETAIL PRICE: $525

HERE'S LOOKING AT YOU, KITTY
Warner Bros. Limited Editions
STYLE NO. WB1029
EDITION SIZE: 250, CEL SIZE: 12F
ORIGINAL RETAIL PRICE: $450

THE LEGENDARY BIG MAN
Warner Bros. Limited Editions
STYLE NO. WB1044
EDITION SIZE: 500, CEL SIZE: 16F
ORIGINAL RETAIL PRICE: $950

LET THE GAMES BEGIN
Warner Bros. Limited Editions
STYLE NO. WB1033
EDITION SIZE: 500, CEL SIZE: 16F
ORIGINAL RETAIL PRICE: $450

PEPÉ LE PEW MODEL SHEET
Warner Bros. Limited Editions
STYLE NO. WB1035
EDITION SIZE: 750, CEL SIZE: 16F
ORIGINAL RETAIL PRICE: $525

THE MAN OF STEEL
Warner Bros. Limited Editions
STYLE NO. WB1045
EDITION SIZE: 500, CEL SIZE: 12F
ORIGINAL RETAIL PRICE: $550

PI(E)
Warner Bros. Limited Editions
STYLE NO. WB1026
EDITION SIZE: 500, CEL SIZE: 12F
ORIGINAL RETAIL PRICE: $400

SPACE JAM
Warner Bros. Limited Editions
STYLE NO. WB1046
EDITION SIZE: 500, CEL SIZE: 16F
ORIGINAL RETAIL PRICE: $1,750

MASTERS OF ANIMATION
Warner Bros. Limited Editions
STYLE NO. WB1042
EDITION SIZE: 500, CEL SIZE: (special)
ORIGINAL RETAIL PRICE: $950

STAR TRUCK
Warner Bros. Limited Editions
STYLE NO. WB1037
EDITION SIZE: 500, CEL SIZE: 12F
ORIGINAL RETAIL PRICE: $425

"... MOTHER! ..."
Warner Bros. Limited Editions
STYLE NO. WB1043
EDITION SIZE: 500, CEL SIZE: (demi)
ORIGINAL RETAIL PRICE: $700

TRIBUTE TO FRIZ
Warner Bros. Limited Editions
STYLE NO. WB1025
EDITION SIZE: 500, CEL SIZE: 16F
ORIGINAL RETAIL PRICE: $700

OF ALL THE JUICE JOINTS
Warner Bros. Limited Editions
STYLE NO. WB1040
EDITION SIZE: 250, CEL SIZE: 12F(pan)
ORIGINAL RETAIL PRICE: $950

WHEN BAT'S AWAY,
    THE GIRLS WILL PLAY
Warner Bros. Limited Editions
STYLE NO. WB1028
EDITION SIZE: 500, CEL SIZE: 12F
ORIGINAL RETAIL PRICE: $400

LET'S PLAY BALL
Warner Bros. Sericels
STYLE NO. SC1033
EDITION SIZE: 2500, CEL SIZE: 12F+
ORIGINAL RETAIL PRICE: $250

"YOU CAN'T ESCAPE ME, DODGERS!"
Warner Bros. Limited Editions
STYLE NO. WB1047
EDITION SIZE: 500, CEL SIZE: 12F
ORIGINAL RETAIL PRICE: $500

OUT OF ORDER
Warner Bros. Sericels
STYLE NO. SC1026
EDITION SIZE: 2500, CEL SIZE: 12F
ORIGINAL RETAIL PRICE: $175

DRINK UP PUDDY TAT
Warner Bros. Sericels
STYLE NO. SC1027
EDITION SIZE: 2500, CEL SIZE: 12F
ORIGINAL RETAIL PRICE: $175

PEPÉ LE PEW LOVES YOU
Warner Bros. Sericels
STYLE NO. SC1028
EDITION SIZE: 2500, CEL SIZE: 12F
ORIGINAL RETAIL PRICE: $175

DUCK DODGERS IN THE 24 1/2 CENTURY
Warner Bros. Sericels
STYLE NO. SC1030
EDITION SIZE: 5000, CEL SIZE: (pan)
ORIGINAL RETAIL PRICE: $185

POP 'IM POP
Warner Bros. Sericels
STYLE NO. SC1034
EDITION SIZE: 2500, CEL SIZE: 12F
ORIGINAL RETAIL PRICE: $185

TASMANIAN DIVOT
Warner Bros. Sericels
STYLE NO. SC1029
EDITION SIZE: 2500, CEL SIZE: 16F
ORIGINAL RETAIL PRICE: $175

FOOTBALL FOLLIES
Warner Bros. Sericels
STYLE NO. SC1025
EDITION SIZE: 2500, CEL SIZE: 16F
ORIGINAL RETAIL PRICE: $185

Warner Bros. Animation Chronology: 1930 to the Present

1930

January 28. Hugh Harman and Rudolf Ising, former animators for Walt Disney, sign with Leon Schlesinger, a manufacturer of silent film main title and dialogue cards. The animators begin producing Looney Tunes cartoons, which will be distributed to theaters by Schlesinger's friends the Warner brothers, whose movie studio bears their name.

Harman and Ising begin hiring former Disney artists and animators, including Isadore "Friz" Freleng.

May. *Sinkin' In The Bathtub* (Looney Tunes), directed by Harman and Ising and drawn by Freleng, debuts. The film stars Bosko and his girl, Honey.

1931

Lady Play Your Mandolin, the first of the Merrie Melodies series, debuts. Produced and directed by Rudolf Ising and drawn by Rollin Hamilton and Norm Blackburn, the cartoon features Foxy, who, at the end of the short, jumps from behind a drum and shouts, "So long, folks!"

1933

Harman and Ising leave Leon Schlesinger Productions and begin producing cartoons for rival MGM.

Buddy, a new Looney Tunes character, is created by director Tom Palmer for the short *Buddy's Day Out*.

1934

January 13. *Buddy The Gob* (Looney Tunes), directed by Friz Freleng, animated by Jack King and Ben Clopton. Freleng receives his first on-screen credit as the "supervisor" of this short.

February 17. *Honeymoon Hotel* is the first Merrie Melodies to be produced in color, directed by Earl Duvall, animated by Jack King and Frank Tipper. Looney Tunes cartoons will not be in color for another ten years.

1935

March 2. Porky Pig debuts in *I Haven't Got A Hat* (Merrie Melodies), directed by Friz Freleng, animated by Rollin Hamilton and Jack King. Porky, voiced by Joe Dougherty, displays his stutter during a torturous recitation of "The Midnight Ride of Paul Revere."

Schlesinger hires Fred "Tex" Avery, a Dallas cartoonist who had been working for Walter Lantz, as a supervisor for Merrie Melodies. Chuck Jones and Bob Clampett are assigned to Avery's animation unit, which is housed in a dreary bungalow the animators call "Termite Terrace."

1936

January 11. The trademark Warner Bros. Animation "bull's-eye" makes its first appearance on *I Wanna Play House* (Merrie Melodies), directed by Friz Freleng, animated by Cal Dalton and Sandy Walker.

Radio actor Mel Blanc and musical director Carl Stalling join the Warner Bros. animation team.

Gold Diggers of '49 is the first Tex Avery Looney Tunes, animated by Chuck Jones and Bob Clampett, with appearances by Porky Pig, Beans, and Little Kitty.

1937

April 17. Daffy Duck explodes into cartoons in *Porky's Duck Hunt* (Looney Tunes), directed by Tex Avery, animated by Bob Clampett, Virgil Ross and Robert Cannon.

July 17. *Egghead Rides Again* (Merrie Melodies), directed by Tex Avery. Egghead debuts in this cartoon.

July 24. Clampett directs his first cartoon, *Porky's Badtime Story*, animated by Chuck Jones.

Freleng leaves Warner Bros. to direct cartoons for MGM. He returns a little over a year later.

1938

September 24. *Porky in Wackyland* (Looney Tunes), directed by Bob Clampett, animated by Norm McCabe and I. Ellis. Porky chases the elusive Do-do Bird through Wackyland in this landmark short.

November 19. Chuck Jones's first directing job, *The Night Watchman* (Merrie Melodies), is released. The story is by Tedd Pierce, animated by Ken Harris.

1939

May 20. Sniffles the mouse is introduced in *Naughty but Mice* (Merrie Melodies), directed by Chuck Jones, story by Rich Hogan, animated by Phil Monroe.

1940

May 18. The first attempt to merge animation with live action through an entire cartoon is made in the breakthrough film *You Ought To Be In Pictures* (Looney Tunes), directed by Friz Freleng, story by Jack Miller, animated by Herman Cohen.

July 27. *A Wild Hare* (Merrie Melodies), directed by Tex Avery, story by Rich Hogan, animated by Virgil Ross. The cartoon is the first appearance of Bugs Bunny, who turns audiences into *fans* in this, his breakthrough role.

1941

March 15. *Tortoise Beats Hare* (Merrie Melodies), directed by Tex Avery, story by Dave Monahan, animated by Charles McKimson. Cecil Turtle debuts in this short, and along with his friends and family, pulls a fast one on Bugs.

March 29. *Goofy Groceries* (Merrie Melodies), directed by Bob Clampett (his first color short), story by Melvin Millar, animated by Vive Risto. Super Guy (Merrie Melodies), send-up of the man of steel, makes an appearance months before the classic Max Fleisher *Superman* series finally debuts. Fifty-five years later, Superman would reappear in a Warner Bros. animated series for television.

Tex Avery leaves the studio after he has a dispute with Schlesinger over cutting off the end of his film *The Heckling Hare*, which featured film history's longest fall and starred Bugs Bunny and the dog, Willoughby.

Bob Clampett takes over Tex Avery's animation unit.

1942

March 14. *Crazy Cruise*, featuring a brief cameo by Bugs Bunny, is released. The short was begun by Tex Avery and was finished by Bob Clampett.

March. *Any Bonds Today?*, directed by Bob Clampett, sponsored by the U.S. Government. Schlesinger rushed this two-minute short into theaters following the attack on Pearl Harbor three months earlier. The cartoon was a plea to theatergoers to buy war bonds.

April 11. *Horton Hatches The Egg* (Merrie Melodies), based on the children's book by Theodore Geisel (Dr. Seuss), was directed by Bob Clampett and animated by Robert McKimson. *Horton Hatches The Egg* is the only Warner Bros. cartoon to be adapted from a book.

July 11. Beaky Buzzard makes his screen debut alongside Bugs Bunny in *Bugs Bunny Gets The Boid* (Merrie Melodies), directed by Bob Clampett, story by Warren Foster, animated by Rod Scribner.

October 3. The first color Looney Tunes is *The Hep Cat*, directed by Bob Clampett, story by Warren Foster, animated by Robert McKimson.

November 21. "I tawt I taw a Puddy Tat!" is first used in *A Tale of Two Kitties* (Merrie Melodies). Directed by Bob Clampett and animated by Robert McKimson and Rod Scribner.

1943
January 16. Despite its blatant racial stereotyping, *Coal Black and de Sebben Dwarfs* is considered by many animation buffs to be one of the greatest cartoons of all time. This Merrie Melodies' lively, hilarious pacing and action was directed by Bob Clampett, story by Warren Foster, animated by Rod Scribner.

Robert McKimson, under Bob Clampett's direction, redefines Bugs Bunny's "look" in the now-legendary model sheet, evolving the rabbit into the familiar character we know today.

June. The first of twenty-six "Pvt. Snafu" cartoons is released, to be shown at U.S. military bases. Directed alternately by Chuck Jones, Friz Freleng, Bob Clampett, and Frank Tashlin, the cartoons depict the *worst* soldier in the Army, and offer funny lessons on what *not* to do to stay alive. Many of the scripts are written by Theodore Geisel (Dr. Seuss).

September 18. Spoofing Disney's epic *Fantasia*, Schlesinger presents *A Corny Concerto* (Merrie Melodies), directed by Bob Clampett, story by Frank Tashlin, animated by Robert McKimson. Bugs Bunny, Elmer Fudd, Porky Pig, and a family of swans are featured in this witty parody.

December 11. The last of the black-and-white Looney Tunes is *Puss n' Booty*, directed by Frank Tashlin, story by Warren Foster, animated by Cal Dalton.

1944
January 1. *Little Red Riding Rabbit* (Merrie Melodies), story by Michael Maltese, animated by Manuel Perez. In this Freleng short, Bugs is the rabbit that Little Red Riding Hood ("Hey, grandma! That's an awfully big nose for you ta have!") is bringing to dinner. Unfortunately, Grandma is "working the swing shift at Lockheed," leaving Bugs to mix it up with the big, bad wolf.

Leon Schlesinger sells his interest in Looney Tunes and Merrie Melodies to Warner Bros. Jack Warner appoints Edward Selzer producer in charge of the animation department.

February 26. *Bugs Bunny And The Three Bears* (Merrie Melodies), directed by Chuck Jones, story by Tedd Pierce, animated by Robert Cannon. Another classic fable takes a beating, this time at the hands of Bugs and the bears.

August 19. *Birdy and the Beast* (Merrie Melodies), directed by Bob Clampett, story by Warren Foster, animated by Tom McKimson. Tweety becomes the main character for the first time while evading yet another hungry puddy tat.

August 26. *Buckaroo Bugs* (Looney Tunes), directed by Bob Clampett, story by Lou Lilly, animated by Emmanuel Gould. Red Hot Ryder made his debut in this short, the first starring appearance of Bugs Bunny in a Looney Tunes cartoon.

1945
January 6. Pepé Le Pew, the over-amorous skunk, was introduced in *Odor-able Kitty*, a Looney Tunes short

directed by Chuck Jones, story by Tedd Pierce, animated by Robert Cannon.

January 13. *Herr Meets Hare* (Merrie Melodies), directed by Friz Freleng, story by Michael Maltese, animated by Gerry Chiniquy. Bugs Bunny takes on a Nazi officer, probably inspired by Herman Goering, in this wartime offering.

March 24. The famished feline Sylvester makes his debut in *Life With Feathers* (Merrie Melodies), directed by Friz Freleng, story by Tedd Pierce, animated by Virgil Ross. Freleng is nominated for an Academy Award.

May 5. Yosemite Sam blasts his way to stardom in *Hare Trigger* (Merrie Melodies), directed by Friz Freleng, story by Michael Maltese, animated by Manuel Perez, Ken Champin, Virgil Ross, and Gerry Chiniquy. This is the first Warner Bros. cartoon to give full credit to its creative team.

Frank Tashlin leaves Warner Bros., and his animation unit is taken over by Robert McKimson.

1946
April 6. Robert McKimson's first outing as a director is the raucous *Daffy Doodles*, story by Warren Foster. Porky Pig is a police officer whose unenviable task is to catch Daffy Duck, the fiend responsible for painting mustaches on every poster in town.

August 31. A supporting player steals the short in *Wally Talky Hawky* (Merrie Melodies), directed by Robert McKimson. Foghorn (ah-say) Foghorn Leghorn makes his debut here, in what was originally a Henery Hawk short. The giant rooster uses Henery Hawk's determination to catch a chicken as a means for tormenting the barnyard dog.

Bob Clampett leaves Warner Bros., and his animation unit is taken over by Arthur Davis.

November 9. *Rhapsody Rabbit* (Merrie Melodies), directed by Friz Freleng, story by Tedd Pierce and Michael Maltese, animated by Manuel Perez, Ken Champin, Virgil

Ross, and Gerry Chiniquy. In another high point of his career, Bugs is a concert pianist trying to deliver a recital despite the mischief of a scene-stealing mouse.

1947
January 25. *The Goofy Gophers* (Looney Tunes), directed by Arthur Davis. Mac and Tosh, the insufferably polite gophers, make their debuts in this short, in which they try to outsmart a guard dog and ransack a vegetable garden. Bugs Bunny makes a cameo appearance.

March 22. *A Hare Grows in Manhattan* (Merrie Melodies), directed by Friz Freleng, story by Michael Maltese and Tedd Pierce, animated by Virgil Ross, Gerry Chiniquy, Manuel Perez, and Ken Champin. Now an established star with a long string of hit cartoons, Bugs recounts his own "story," in which he grew up on the lower east side and outsmarted a pack of canine ruffians.

May 3. *Tweetie Pie* features the debut of Tweety and Sylvester as a team in a Merrie Melodies directed by Friz Freleng. During production of this short, producer Edward Selzer orders Freleng to use a woodpecker from an earlier film instead of a canary; Freleng hands Selzer his pencil and quits. That night, Freleng is called at home and rehired by a conciliatory Selzer. When the short wins Warner Bros. Animation's first Academy Award the following March, Selzer accepts the statuette.

November 1. *Slick Hare* (Merrie Melodies), directed by Friz Freleng, story by Michael Maltese and Tedd Pierce, animated by Virgil Ross, Gerry Chiniquy, Manuel Perez, and Ken Champin. One of several cartoons in which Bugs and Elmer co-star with caricatures of the era's greatest screen stars, including Humphrey Bogart, Gregory Peck, Frank Sinatra, Sidney Greenstreet, Carmen Miranda, and Lauren Bacall.

1948
January 3. *Gorilla My Dreams* (Looney Tunes), directed by Robert McKimson, story by Warren Foster, animated by Charles McKimson, Manny Gould, and John Carey.

Gruesome Gorilla debuts as Bugs's unwilling foster father after the rabbit is "adopted" by Mrs. Gorilla.

March 27. *Back Alley Oproar* (Merrie Melodies), directed by Friz Freleng, story by Michael Maltese and Tedd Pierce, animated by Gerry Chiniquy, Manuel Perez, Ken Champin, and Virgil Ross. A standout performance by Sylvester the Cat, who performs a series of moonlit arias, interrupting the sleep of a weary Elmer Fudd.

April 10. *Rabbit Punch* (Merrie Melodies), directed by Chuck Jones, story by Tedd Pierce and Michael Maltese, animated by Phil Monroe, Ken Harris, Lloyd Vaughan, and Ben Washam. After heckling "the champ," Bugs finds himself in the boxing ring in this, the first of many "Bugs vs. an overwhelming opponent" shorts.

May 8. *Buccaneer Bunny* (Looney Tunes), directed by Friz Freleng, story by Michael Maltese and Tedd Pierce, animated by Manuel Perez, Ken Champin, Virgil Ross, and Gerry Chiniquy. Yosemite Sam is transformed into a pirate in this outing, which sets the tone for subsequent Bugs vs. Sam shorts.

July 24. "Surrender, Earthling!" Clad in a tutu and a Roman helmet and armed with the dreaded "Illudium Pew 36 Space Modulator," Marvin The Martian (initially known as "Commander X-2") makes his debut in *Haredevil Hare*, a Looney Tunes directed by Chuck Jones, story by Michael Maltese, animated by Ben Washam, Lloyd Vaughan, Ken Harris, and Phil Monroe.

1949
September 16. *Fast and Furry-ous* introduces Road Runner and Wile E. Coyote. This Looney Tunes cartoon, directed by Chuck Jones, story by Michael Maltese, animated by Ken Harris, Phil Monroe, Lloyd Vaughan, and Ben Washam, establishes the formula for the duo's future vehicles: a series of unrelated blackouts in which the coyote (*Carnivorous vulgaris*) employs a variety of outlandish schemes and devices in his unsuccessful pursuit of his prey (*Accelleratii incredibus*). The pair become the center of one of Warner

Bros.' most popular series of shorts for the next decade.

November 12. *For Scent-imental Reasons* (Looney Tunes), directed by Chuck Jones, story by Michael Maltese, animated by Ben Washam, Ken Harris, Phil Monroe, and Lloyd Vaughan. This installment in the adventures of the love-struck Pepé Le Pew and the elusive feline object of his desire brings home Warner Bros. Animation's second Oscar.

December 24. *Rabbit Hood* (Merrie Melodies), directed by Chuck Jones, story by Michael Maltese, animated by Ken Harris, Phil Monroe, Ben Washam, and Lloyd Vaughan. In a clip from his most famous film, Errol Flynn makes a cameo as Bugs outsmarts the Sheriff of Nottingham. In exchange for the right to use his image, a flattered Flynn requests only a copy of the cartoon for his collection.

December 25. Leon Schlesinger dies.

1950
March 4. *The Scarlet Pumpernickel* (Looney Tunes), directed by Chuck Jones, story by Michael Maltese, animated by Phil Monroe, Ben Washam, Lloyd Vaughan, and Ken Harris. One of Daffy Duck's signature films co-stars many of the studio's most famous characters, including Sylvester the Cat, Porky Pig, Mama Bear, Henery Hawk, and Elmer Fudd.

Chuck Jones wins his second Oscar for *So Much For So Little*, an educational film released in theaters, promoting the U.S. Public Health Service.

October 7. Granny makes her debut as Tweety's doting owner in *Canary Row* (Merrie Melodies), directed by Friz Freleng, story by Tedd Pierce, animated by Art Davis, Ken Champin, Virgil Ross, Emery Hawkings, and Gerry Chiniquy.

October 28. *Pop 'Im Pop!*, a Looney Tunes directed by Robert McKimson. Sylvester Jr. debuts as Sylvester the Cat's anguished son, who laments the fact that Dad can't fight a giant mouse (who, unbeknownst to them, is actually Gracie, the Fighting Kangaroo).

December 16. *Rabbit of Seville* (Looney Tunes), directed by Chuck Jones, story by Michael Maltese. Bugs Bunny's and Elmer Fudd's takes on Rossini's famous *Il Barbiere Di Siviglia* is a Jones classic.

1951
March 10. *Bunny Hugged* (Merrie Melodies), directed by Chuck Jones, story by Michael Maltese, animated by Ken Harris, Phil Monroe, Ben Washam, and Lloyd Vaughan. Bugs, the mascot of "Ravishing Ronald," finds himself in the wrestling ring after his fighter is quickly dispatched by "The Crusher."

May 19. *Rabbit Fire* (Looney Tunes), directed by Chuck Jones, story by Michael Maltese, animated by Lloyd Vaughan, Ken Harris, Phil Monroe, and Ben Washam. The first of an unintentional cartoon trilogy in which Bugs and Daffy argue over whether it's really Duck Season or Rabbit Season. Fortunately for them, it turns out to be Elmer Season. With Maltese's wit and wordplay, and Jones's extraordinary direction, the three cartoons take the characters to a new level of sophistication. The short also establishes Daffy as a character with as many psychological shadings as Bugs.

Dwindling budgets and the influence of the style of UPA (United Productions of America), an independent studio, change the look of the Warner Bros. cartoons. The shorts, while still maintaining their comedic snap and satirical vigor, begin to feature dramatically stylized backgrounds, a trademark of UPA cartoons.

1952
January 19. *Operation: Rabbit* (Looney Tunes), directed by Chuck Jones, story by Michael Maltese, animated by Lloyd Vaughan, Ben Washam, Ken Harris, and Phil Monroe. Wile E. Coyote, now a "super genius," matches wits with Bugs Bunny for the first time in this cartoon.

February 2. Pussyfoot, the adorable kitten who attaches herself to Marc Antony the bulldog, is featured in *Feed the Kitty (Merrie Melodies),*

directed by Chuck Jones, story by Michael Maltese, animated by Ken Harris, Phil Monroe, Lloyd Vaughan, and Ben Washam.

September 20. *Rabbit Seasoning* (Merrie Melodies), directed by Chuck Jones, story by Michael Maltese, animated by Ben Washam, Lloyd Vaughan, and Ken Harris. The second of Jones's three "Rabbit Season/Duck Season" shorts. This one ends with what would become Daffy's catchphrase: "You're despicable!"

November 15. Pete Puma makes his first appearance a memorable one in *Rabbit's Kin* (Merrie Melodies), directed by Robert McKimson, story by Tedd Pierce, animated by Charles McKimson, Herman Cohen, Rod Scribner, and Phil De Lara.

1953
January 3. Ralph Wolf and Sam the Sheepdog are introduced as clock-punching adversaries who put in a full day's work around a flock of sheep in *Don't Give Up The Sheep* (Looney Tunes), directed by Chuck Jones, story by Michael Maltese, animated by Ken Harris, Ben Washam, and Lloyd Vaughan.

February 28. *Duck Amuck* (Merrie Melodies), directed by Chuck Jones, story by Michael Maltese, animated by Ken Harris, Ben Washam, and Lloyd Vaughan. Daffy Duck meets his maker, an off-screen, unseen animator who torments the duck by constantly redrawing his backgrounds and, finally, Daffy himself.

July 25. *Duck Dodgers in the 24 1/2th Century* (Merrie Melodies), directed by Chuck Jones, story by Michael Maltese, animated by Ben Washam, Lloyd Vaughan, and Ken Harris. One of Daffy's greatest outings, this one co-stars Porky Pig (as the Eager Young Space Cadet), and Marvin the Martian in a race to discover a new source for Illudium Phosdex (the shaving cream atom).

August 29. Speedy Gonzales, "the fastest mouse in all of Mexico," tears across the screen in *Cat-Tails for Two*, a Merrie Melodies directed by Robert McKimson, story by Tedd Pierce, animated by Rod Scribner, Phil De Lara, Charles McKimson, and Herman Cohen.

October 3. *Duck! Rabbit, Duck!*, a Merrie Melodies directed by Chuck Jones, story by Michael Maltese, animated by Ken Harris, Ben Washam, Lloyd Vaughan, Richard Thompson, and Abe Levitow. The third of the "Rabbit Season/Duck Season" trilogy. This time, it turns out to be Baseball Season, sending Elmer on a hunt for baseballs.

1954
March 13. *Bugs and Thugs* (Looney Tunes), directed by Friz Freleng, story by Warren Foster, animated by Manuel Perez, Ken Champin, Virgil Ross, and Art Davis. Mugsy, one of a pair of 1930s-style gangsters, makes his debut in this piece, in which they kidnap Bugs. Rocky appears first in 1950's *Golden Yeggs*. In the end, though, it's the rabbit who ends up taking them for a ride.

June 19. The twirling, chomping, growling Tasmanian Devil debuts in *Devil May Hare* (Looney Tunes), directed by Robert McKimson, story by Sid Marcus, animated by Herman Cohen, Rod Scribner, Phil De Lara, and Charles McKimson.

July 24. The bedeviling Witch Hazel is introduced in *Bewitched Bunny* (Looney Tunes), directed by Chuck Jones, story by Michael Maltese, animated by Lloyd Vaughan, Ken Harris, and Ben Washam.

December 18. *Baby Buggy Bunny* (Merrie Melodies), directed by Chuck Jones, story by Michael Maltese, animated by Abe Levitow, Ken Harris, and Ben Washam. Baby Faced Finster (alias Ant Hill Harry), makes a memorable appearance as a bank robber who nearly gets the best of Bugs.

1955
September 17. Freleng wins his second Oscar for *Speedy Gonzales* (Merrie Melodies), with story by Warren Foster, animated by Gerry Chiniquy, Ted Bonnicksen, and Art Davis.

December 31. *One Froggy Evening* (Merrie Melodies), directed by Chuck Jones, story by Michael Maltese, animated by Abe Levitow, Richard Thompson, Ken Harris, and Ben Washam. Michigan J. Frog's appearance in this short is so memorable that nearly forty years later he would become the mascot for the Warner Bros. Television Network. His rendition of "Hello My Ragtime Gal" is one of the most recognizable tunes in film history.

The Warner animation team from Hollywood moves to new studios on the Warner Bros. Burbank lot.

1956
May 5. *Gee Whiz-z-z-z-z-z* (Looney Tunes), directed by Chuck Jones, story by Michael Maltese, animated by Abe Levitow, Ben Washam, Richard Thompson, and Ken Harris. The short features such classic gags as the "Acme Bat-man Outfit" and a painting of a bridge that's an actual bridge for Road Runner, but merely a painting for the Coyote.

In a move that would introduce Warner Bros. cartoons to a new generation and insure their permanent place in American culture, the company sells all pre-1948 color cartoons to Associated Artists Productions (AAP) for TV syndication. Bugs Bunny, Daffy Duck, and friends become an after-school staple for millions of American children.

1957
January 5. *Three Little Bops* (Looney Tunes), directed by Friz Freleng, story by Warren Foster, narrated by Stan Freberg. The story of the Three Little Pigs is retold in modern jazz in one of Freleng's best.

July 6. *What's Opera, Doc?*, a Merrie Melodies directed by Chuck Jones, story by Michael Maltese, animated by Ken Harris, Abe Levitow, and Richard Thompson. Jones's crew, along with musical director Milt Franklyn, bend and compress Wagner's *Ring* cycle into a seven-minute classic. In 1992, the short is inducted by Congress into the National Film Registry as a bona fide

film classic, one of a handful of cartoons to be awarded the honor.

August 10. *Birds Anonymous* (Merrie Melodies), directed by Friz Freleng. Sylvester becomes the first Hollywood star to turn himself in to a twelve-step program in this cartoon, which won Freleng his third Academy Award.

1958
Edward Selzer, executive producer of the cartoon division since the studio was bought from Leon Schlesinger, retires and is replaced by John Burton.

August 23. When Bugs rescued the "Singing Sword" from The Black Knight (Yosemite Sam) in Looney Tunes' *Knighty Knight Bugs*, he also captured his first Oscar (the fourth for Freleng).

1959
January 10. *Baton Bunny* (Looney Tunes), directed by Chuck Jones, story by Michael Maltese, animated by Ken Harris, Richard Thompson, and Ben Washam. Bugs leads the orchestra through Franz von Suppe's *Morning, Noon, and Night in Vienna* and single-handedly plays the roles of cowboys, Indians, and cavalry.

Arthur Q. Bryan, the voice of Elmer Fudd, dies.

1960
Cartoon Division Executive Producer John Burton leaves Warner Bros. David DePatie steps in as studio leader.

October 1. "The Bugs Bunny Show" debuts on ABC in prime time. After it's moved to its now-familiar Saturday morning slot in 1962, it becomes the longest-running Saturday morning children's show in television history.

December 3. *High Note* (Looney Tunes), directed by Chuck Jones. A drunken musical note is the star of this short, which didn't contain a word of dialogue. The film garners an Academy Award nomination for Jones.

Film attendance, and with it the demand for theatrical cartoons, drops as television strengthens its foothold in American homes.

1964
August 1. *Senorella and the Glass Huarache*, a Looney Tunes short directed by Hawley Pratt, story by John Dunn, animated by Gerry Chiniquy, Virgil Ross, Bob Matz, and Lee Halpern, is released. This will be last theatrical short from the classic studio until 1987.

Friz Freleng and David DePatie lease Warners' cartoon plant and establish DePatie-Freleng Enterprises Inc. They make 37 cartoons under the Warner Bros. shield.

1967
The success of DePatie-Freleng gets Jack Warner's attention, and he reopens the cartoon studio off the Warner lot.

1969
Warner Bros. discontinues distribution of all short subjects, and the revived studio is, for the time being, closed.

1975
As renewed interest in the old cartoons grows, screenings and tributes are held worldwide.

"The Boys from Termite Terrace," a documentary by John Canemaker about the old cartoon studio, is broadcast on CBS, setting off a wave of inquiries about the studio and reawakening interest in the history of Warner Bros. Animation.

A feature film, *Bugs Bunny: Superstar*, featuring interviews with Avery, Clampett, and Freleng, as well as a selection of pre-1948 cartoons and home movies of the old studio, is released in theaters. Narrated by Orson Welles, the film earns rave reviews.

1976–1979
November 1976: *Carnival of the Animals*, directed by Chuck Jones and featuring the music of Camille

Saint-Saens and the poetry of Ogden Nash, launches a series of half-hour compilation specials for prime-time broadcast. They are enthusiastically received by viewers. More than twenty similar specials are produced over the next fifteen years.

1979

September 29. *The Bugs Bunny/Road Runner Movie* (called "The Great American Chase"), a theatrical release of assembled clips from Chuck Jones's old Warner Bros. cartoons (and twenty minutes of new animation), is selected to open the 1979 New York Film Festival before being released nationally.

1980

Friz Freleng is named executive producer of the revived cartoon division at Warner Bros., a studio response to the steady interest in the animated characters. Filled with young, newly hired animators, the studio creates TV, theatrical, and commercial projects.

1981

November 20. *Friz Freleng's Looney Looney Looney Bugs Bunny Movie* is released.

1982

November 19. *Bugs Bunny's 3rd Movie: 1001 Rabbit Tales*, directed by Friz Freleng, is released.

1983

August 5. *Daffy Duck's Movie: Fantastic Island*, another Freleng production, is released.

1985

December 21. Bugs Bunny receives a star on the Hollywood Walk of Fame on Hollywood Boulevard. The ceremony is attended by Friz Freleng, Chuck Jones, Bugs, and hundreds of fans.

1987

April. Bugs Bunny (assisted by Tom Hanks) presents the Oscar for Best Animated Short Subject on the 1987 Academy Awards show.

November 20. Warner Bros. Animation produces *The Duxorcist*, the first theatrical cartoon out of the studio in almost two decades. The short is directed by Greg Ford and Terry Lennon.

1988

September 23. *Night of the Living Duck*, a Daffy Duck theatrical short, premieres at the New York Film Festival. Directed by Ford and Lennon, it features Mel Torme voicing Daffy's singing in a nightclub lounge, along with Mel Blanc's last cartoon work.

September 24. *Daffy Duck's Quackbusters*, a feature-length film directed by Ford and Lennon, is released. The film features a compilation of old footage and new animation.

1989

July. Mel Blanc, who provided a voice for the bulk of Warner Bros.' cartoon characters for more than fifty years, dies.

1990

September. "Steven Spielberg's Tiny Toon Adventures" debuts. The show features pint-sized pupils of the legendary Looney Tunes repertory company. Produced by Tom Ruegger and Jean MacCurdy for Warner's new television division, the show would be the first of several to gather twenty Emmy Awards (including Best Animated Series, Best Writing, and Best Music) for the animation studio.

November 2. *Box Office Bunny*, directed by Darrell Van Citters, is the first Bugs Bunny big-screen short in twenty-six years. The cartoon co-stars Daffy Duck and Elmer Fudd, and is released to coincide with the year-long celebration of the 50th birthday of Bugs Bunny.

1991

Bugs again presents the Oscar for Best Animated Short Subject during the Academy Award ceremonies.

Warner Bros. Animation produces "Taz-Mania," a half-hour series based on the daily life of the irrepressible Tasmanian Devil and his family.

1992

January. "Hare Jordan," the innovative Nike Super Bowl commercial starring Michael Jordan and Bugs Bunny, is telecast. It later wins numerous commercial awards, setting the stage for a theatrical teaming of Bugs and Jordan.

August. Friz Freleng receives his star on the Hollywood Walk of Fame.

October. "Batman: The Animated Series" makes its debut. Based on the style and characters of the original Bob Kane comics, the series is a hit with both kids and adult reviewers.

1993

September. "Steven Spielberg Presents Animaniacs" debuts on afternoon television. The series, headlined by Yakko, Wakko, and Dot Warner, is the most successful latter-day attempt to recapture the lunacy and satirical edge of the classic Warner Bros. cartoons. Other Animaniacs include Pinky and the Brain, the Goodfeathers, and Slappy Squirrel. The show will win numerous Emmys and a Peabody Award.

November. *Chariots of Fur*, starring the Road Runner and the Coyote, is released. Directed by Chuck Jones.

1995

January 11. Michigan J. Frog and Chuck Jones throw the power switch to launch Warner Bros. new network, The WB.

February. Chuck Jones receives a star on the Hollywood Walk of Fame.

April. Once more, Bugs Bunny (this time assisted by Daffy Duck) presents an Oscar.

August 25. *Carrotblanca*, a spoof of *Casablanca*, is released nationally. Directed by Doug McCarthy and assistant director Spike Brandt, the film stars a crowd of Looney Tunes characters.

September. "Steven Spielberg Presents Pinky and the Brain" debuts in prime time on the fledgling Warner Bros. Television Network (promoted by mascot Michigan J. Frog as "The WB").

"The Sylvester and Tweety Mysteries" makes its debut on the Kids WB! on Saturday mornings, along with "Steven Spielberg Presents Freakazoid!"

1996

June. Warner Bros. Movie World in Bottrop, Germany premieres the landmark animated 3-D film *Marvin Der Marsmench In Der Dritten Dimension* (*Marvin The Martian in the Third Dimension*). The film is shown in New York at the studio's flagship studio store in October.

September. "Superman," a new animated series, debuts on The WB. The series combines the visual styles of Warner Bros.' new "Batman" series and the classic Max Fleischer short subjects of the 1940s.

Superior Duck, starring Daffy Duck, is released. Directed by Chuck Jones.

November 15. *Space Jam*, the first feature-length film starring the Looney Tunes characters (with basketball legend Michael Jordan), is released.

1997

December. Warner Bros. Movie World in Oxenford-Gold Coast, Australia premieres the animated 3-D film "Marvin The Martian in the Third Dimension" to rave reviews making it one of the most visited attractions in the park.

Index

Page numbers in *italics* indicate illustrations.

½ EYE WIDTH
BETWEEN EYES

BILL FLEXIBLE
FOR DIALOGUE
SHAPES

APPROXIMATELY
4 HEADS HIGH

WHITE OF BELLY
CONTINUES THRU
TO TAIL

LONG HANDS
AND FINGERS

DRAW EARS AND WHISKERS
TO SUIT MOOD

HEIGHT VARIES WITH POSE
PROPORTIONS DO NOT

FANNY
PROTRUDES
FROM BODY
SHAPE

NOSE AND EYES FIT SHAPE OF HEAD

LARGE
FLAT FEET

BILL ABOUT
TWO HEADS LONG

RING ON
NECK

LONG
SKINNY NECK

KEEP RUFF
ON CHEEKS HIGH
IT MAKES HIM
YOUNGER

KEEP NECK
FAIRLY SHORT

ARMS
AT W

LARGE
FLAT FEET

DAFFY DUCK

BUGS BUNNY

LAST HAIR
LONGEST

BABY STARE

TUCK BOW TIE
UNDER CHIN

JAW AREA ABO
HEIGHT OF HEAD

ET AND
S DIFFERENT
OR THAN
DY

APPROX. 1½ EYE
WIDTH BETWEEN EYES

CHEEKS
DROOP A BIT

DON'T DRAW
TOO TALL

1

TE HAIR
AILS AND
NGTH

½   ¾

CUTE
COMPACT
SNOUT

NO NECK

NOTE SIZE
OF PUPIL

2½ HEADS HIGH

BROWS HIGH
ON FOREHEAD

CARRY
TAIL HIGH
ON FANNY

FIRST HAIR
SHORTEST

HAS HANDS
WHEN NEEDED

NO TEETH!

CURLY Q
TAIL

PORKY

"TWEETY"

KEEP
TWEETY
COMPACT